THE SOVIET BUREAUCRATIC ELITE

A Case Study of the
Ukrainian Apparatus

by John A. Armstrong

Today, the top echelon of Soviet leaders is the subject of almost daily attention in the world press. But what of the officials just below them in the huge bureaucracy which controls the U.S.S.R.? Important both as lieutenants of the top leaders and as men who, in the shifting alignments of Soviet politics, may themselves reach the top, these officials have received relatively little attention.

THE SOVIET BUREAUCRATIC ELITE, which is based on an intensive study of the Ukrainian apparatus since the Great Purge of the thirties, fills this important gap. Using numerous individual examples combined with detailed statistical analyses, the author describes the background characteristics, the career patterns, and the rate of turnover of officials within many categories of the Soviet bureaucracy.

Along with his exhaustive analysis of a great mass of hitherto obscure information from the Ukrainian press, Dr. Armstrong introduces a considerable amount of comparative material from general Soviet publications and from the local press in other areas. In addition, during two recent visits to the U.S.S.R., he obtained access to a number of unpublished academic dissertations dealing with the Ukrainian and the Soviet apparatus, giving him a truly unique fund of source material.

The result is a study whic[h] the usual monograph. THI[S] REAUCRATIC ELITE rev[eals] divergencies among various the Party, as well as betwee[n] other power elements. It sug[gests] of generations" between the officials who secured high posts after the Purge and those officials who comprise the newer group; it

(continued on back flap)

THE SOVIET BUREAUCRATIC ELITE

A Case Study of the Ukrainian Apparatus

By JOHN A. ARMSTRONG

FREDERICK A. PRAEGER, *Publishers*
NEW YORK

BOOKS THAT MATTER

FIRST PUBLISHED IN THE UNITED STATES OF AMERICA IN 1959
BY FREDERICK A. PRAEGER, INC., PUBLISHERS
15 WEST 47TH STREET, NEW YORK 36, N. Y.

© 1959 in the United States of America
by FREDERICK A. PRAEGER, INC.

Library of Congress catalog card number 59–7887

Printed in the United States of America

THIS BOOK IS NUMBER 76 OF

PRAEGER PUBLICATIONS IN RUSSIAN HISTORY AND WORLD COMMUNISM

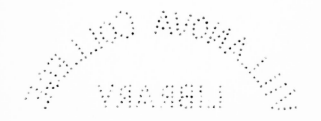

To my Parents

Acknowledgments

I N UNDERTAKING an intensive specialized study like that contained in this book, the scholar is in many ways dependent upon the advice and encouragement of his colleagues. I have indeed been fortunate in this respect, though I must, of course, accept full responsibility for the final product. From the beginning, Philip E. Mosely, Director of Studies of the Council on Foreign Relations, was helpful in innumerable ways. Merle Fainsod, Professor of Government of Harvard University, suggested many important improvements after reading the initial draft. My colleagues of the Department of Political Science of the University of Wisconsin were most helpful, especially James E. McCamy, who offered many valuable suggestions based on his long study of administrative machinery.

The bulk of the work was done in the New York Public Library and the Library of Congress. To the staffs of these two great libraries, and especially to Sergius Yakobson and Fritz T. Epstein of the Slavic and Central European Division of the Library of Congress, I am very grateful. The staff of the Lenin State Library, Moscow, was very helpful in providing the dissertations which form part of the source material. While it is impossible to list all those who provided items of information, the associates of the Ukrainian Academy of Arts and Sciences in the United States were especially helpful.

A summer salary grant from the University of Wisconsin and a grant from the Research Program on the History of the Communist Party of the Soviet Union helped me to find the time necessary to complete the study, while the Inter-University Committee on Travel Grants made possible a trip to Moscow, where I obtained much material. A generous subsidy from the Social Science Research Council facilitated publication.

The capable advice of John Haverstick helped me greatly in preparing the final version; to him and the other members of the editorial staff of Frederick A. Praeger, Inc., I am very grateful indeed. Last, but most important, I have been both assisted and encouraged throughout by my wife, Annette Taylor Armstrong.

J. A. A.

Contents

Chapter

THE SOVIET BUREAUCRATIC ELITE

1

Identifying the Decision-Makers

A<small>T FIRST GLANCE</small> the concept of "a Soviet elite" may seem a contradiction in terms. Two major objections can be raised to the concept. First, the present Soviet society is officially described as "classless." Many Western scholars would be very skeptical of this description even on purely theoretical grounds, believing with Karl Mannheim that "the masses always take the form which the creative minorities controlling societies choose to give them."[1] A close inspection of the statements of Soviet leaders indicates, however, that they do not take "classlessness" to mean real equality of power for all members of the Soviet society.[2] Using typically military figures of speech, Joseph Stalin himself wrote:

> In our Party, if we have in mind its leading strata, there are about 3,000 to 4,000 first-rank leaders whom I would call our Party's corps of generals.
> Then there are about 30,000 to 40,000 middle-rank leaders who are our Party's corps of officers.
> Then there are about 100,000 to 150,000 of the lower-rank Party command staff who are, so to speak, our Party's non-commissioned officers.[3]

A second objection to the concept of a Soviet elite is based on the existence of personal dictatorship in the Soviet Union. At its inception the Soviet regime was dominated by Vladimir Lenin's personality, and today Nikita Khrushchev is preeminent among Soviet leaders. Whether or not either of these men should actually be classed as a dictator, there is no doubt that Stalin was an autocratic ruler during most of the period between Lenin's death in 1924 and his own death in 1953—a period which comprised three-quarters of the entire history of the Soviet state. Moreover, after the Great Purge of the middle thirties, when he destroyed almost the entire higher echelon of Soviet officials, Stalin's power was nearly unchecked.

Even an absolute dictator needs lieutenants, however. As the social theorist Vilfredo Pareto pointed out, these lieutenants are frequently more important than the ruler:

> A governing class is present everywhere, even where there is a despot, but the forms under which it appears are widely variable. . . . There are always people who play a very important part in actual government. To be sure they must now and again bend the knee to the whims of ignorant and domineering sovereigns and parliaments, but they are soon back at their tenacious, patient, never-ending work, which is of much the greater consequence.[4]

Still more important, the dictator eventually dies; his subordinates survive him. Since Stalin's death, his former minions have condemned the practice of personal dictatorship and have asserted the primacy of "collective leadership" or group rule:

> One may say without the slightest doubt that the principle of collective leadership has been fully established in the Central Committee. The decision of all the most important questions has passed into the hands of the regularly assembling Plenum of the Central Committee—this broad, collegially functioning Party center, which is most intimately connected to the decisive sections of the structure of Communist society.[5]

Considering Khrushchev's increased power since 1957, one may question the extent to which the Central Committee of the CPSU (The Communist Party of the Soviet Union) regularly exercises "collective leadership." The very fact that Khrushchev was able to defeat his rivals in June, 1957, by appealing to the Central Committee for support indicates, however, its crucial importance at the decisive moment. Today there seems little doubt that the Central Committee is consulted from time to time and that its views are carefully weighed. To this extent, at least, its members share in the exercise of power.

If there is a Soviet elite, how is it constituted? Frequently the examination of the formal institutions of rule is the best approach to the study of an elite. This may be true even in a pluralistic society, where many other channels lead to elite status.[6] As will be shown in Chapter 2, this approach is especially relevant to the study of a totalitarian system like that of the Soviet Union. The role of the Central Committee of the CPSU indicates the importance of institutions in determining membership in the ruling group. As a section of the Communist Party organization, the Central Committee is part of the principal governing institution in the Soviet system. The "decisive sections of the structure of Communist society" which the Central Committee represents also include other institutions, the most important being the state administration, the military officer corps, the police network, and the industrial management. From the sociological standpoint each of these institutions constitutes a highly developed bureaucracy, though Soviet writers prefer to call them, individually or collectively, the "apparatus."[7]

The higher officials of the apparatus constitute the elite, or at least the larger part of the elite. However, it is hard to determine the level at which an official plays a sufficiently important role in decision-making to justify calling him a member of the elite. Given the limitations of our knowledge of the operation of the Soviet system, it would be unwise to attempt a precise definition of this level. In Chapter 2, several Soviet indexes to official status, which may, with reservations, be used as indications of elite membership, will be examined. At this point one should note, however, that both objective consideration of the nature of an elite and the practical requirements of analysis suggest that the elite be defined to include a large, but not enormous, number of members.

The problem of selection of an appropriate group for study will be discussed below. Objectively, it is clear that the pyramidal nature of the Soviet power structure, suggested in Stalin's statement quoted above, limits the size of the elite group. Non-Soviet writers are, therefore, incorrect in referring to the Party membership as the Soviet elite—if "elite" is meant to designate a group which participates to a significant degree in decision-making. The sheer size of the Party membership—nearly 9,000,000 (including "candidates" or probationary members)—militates against such participation. Moreover, a considerable majority of the Party members holds ordinary jobs outside the apparatus altogether. Even the minor officials of the apparatus, numbering several hundred thousand, are obviously not significantly involved in making decisions.

At the other extreme, the Central Committee membership (about 225, again including "candidates"), while undoubtedly part of the ruling group, does not include the entire elite. A fairly broad stratum of officials just below the Central Committee membership shares in the implementation and interpretation of its decisions. In their own spheres of operation these officials make many important decisions, especially those concerning regional and local matters. Moreover, officials at this level constitute the group from which the Central Committee is recruited. This "middle level" of the apparatus is, therefore, extremely significant in the study of the Soviet elite. The next chapter will include a more detailed analysis of the range of this level. First, however, it is important to consider certain practical aspects of studying the Soviet elite.

To a limited extent an analysis of the Soviet elite can utilize data directly presented in Soviet sources. A considerable amount of statistical evidence is published concerning the political elite, especially in connection with the Party Congresses. Since, however, following the wholesale replacement of the elite in 1937-1938, there have been only three Congresses of the CPSU, such evidence is extremely limited for the U.S.S.R. as a whole. Moreover, it must be utilized with great caution, for it is obviously designed in part for propaganda purposes. Much more extensive and less propagandistic data are contained in unpublished studies by Soviet scholars. Some of these are analyses directly related to such features of the elite as the training of higher officials and the rate of circulation in official posts. With rare exceptions, of course, such studies have not been available to Western investigators.[8] Even the unpublished studies must be made within the constrictive framework of Soviet Communist doctrine; consequently, they fail to present very much of the factual information concerning higher officials which the non-Communist scholar desires.

As a result, the investigator of the Soviet political elite is compelled to gather, as well as to analyze, material concerning this group. The principal available method consists of tracing the careers of a large number of elite officials. This laborious procedure is necessary, not only to analyze the background of important individuals but also to provide the basis for statistical computation of such factors as rates of turnover in specific posts and proportions of transfer among official positions. The procedure may also produce important data on the interrelation of the structures of the bureaucratic apparatus itself.

This method presupposes a fairly abundant body of sources which frequently refer to individual elite members at least by name and by position held. In this respect, analysis of the central elite is severely handicapped. As previously suggested, a principal index to this elite is membership in the Central Committee of the CPSU. Membership is announced, however, only when the Committee is elected by the Congress; as mentioned above, only three Congresses of the CPSU have been held since 1938. Moreover, the central press (i.e., the papers and periodicals published in Moscow for the entire Soviet Union) usually provides such an incomplete coverage of officials (other than those at very high levels) that it is very difficult to trace their careers in detail.

At the regional level the situation is quite different. Newspapers and other publications contain relatively abundant references to major officials of the regions.[9] The Central Committees and Congresses of the "Union Republics," which are the major regional subdivisions in much of the U.S.S.R., have met more frequently than have the corresponding bodies for the entire Soviet Union. Moreover, the proceedings of the Republic Party convocations have been reported much more fully than was the case, until very recently, with the Moscow meetings.

For many regions, newspaper and periodical files for the years since 1938—the period of activity of the "post-Purge" elite—are not available outside the U.S.S.R., or are very fragmentary. Even in most of the areas for which sources are available, local conditions differ so much from those of the Union as a whole that the results of analyses of the regional elites could not be readily applied to Soviet conditions in general.

In contrast, the apparatus of the Ukrainian Soviet Republic affords excellent material for a case study. The scope of the Great Purge in this area was enormous, even in comparison with the U.S.S.R. as a whole. Almost one hundred per cent of the higher officials serving in 1937 were replaced by the end of 1938 by persons who had previously been too obscure for public notice. Consequently, the process of tracing the present elite can practically begin with the latter date.[10] While there has been a frequent interchange of lower-level officials between the Ukraine and other parts of the U.S.S.R. since 1938, the middle-level Party and state officials in this region have, as far as it can be determined, been transferred only infrequently to or from other regions.[11] Consequently, the Ukrainian apparatus elite can be studied as a distinct group to a considerable degree.

Sources for the Ukrainian elite are abundant. The two Republic newspapers are available for almost all of the period since 1938, except for the period during which the Ukraine was under German occupation. A number of less important newspapers, books, and memoirs round out the published sources. Some important supplementary data can be obtained from defectors, who were especially numerous from this area, and German occupation documents throw some light on the Soviet apparatus. In addition, Soviet researchers have themselves made a number of significant studies of aspects of the Ukrainian apparatus, although most of these remain as yet unpublished.[12] The Ukrainian press has provided many more background details concerning individual officials and the group as a whole than have appeared in the Moscow press, and still more data are contained in the unpublished studies mentioned above. From 1938 through 1956 six Party Congresses were held for the Ukraine. The meetings of the Central Committee of the Communist Party of the Ukraine (KPU) have been regularly held four times a year; reports of the proceedings, containing the names and positions of the numerous officials speaking on the topics considered, have been frequent. This is in marked contrast to the

CPSU, where Central Committee meetings were not held at all for a long period and where, until Stalin's death, they were rarely reported in detail.[13]

While the Ukrainian elite is easier to examine than is a correspondingly large group for the Soviet Union as a whole, it is obvious that results obtained from such an examination cannot be applied without reservation to the entire ruling group. Certain major bureaucracies are organized entirely on a Union-wide basis; and these, therefore, contain no regional subdivision which can be examined as part of the Ukrainian apparatus. This is most clearly the case with the military. It is true to a lesser extent of the police bureaucracy, which is highly centralized although it does have a definite Ukrainian area of operation. Until very recently, heavy industrial management was also controlled centrally. In all these organizations frequent shifting of personnel between Ukrainian and non-Ukrainian assignments occurs; as a result it is impossible in most cases to make a significant study of career patterns from Ukrainian data alone.

While these major bureaucracies—military, police, and heavy industrial management—are not "of" the Ukrainian apparatus, they nevertheless interact with it. The enormous industrial importance of the Ukraine, the special difficulties encountered in suppressing dissident elements, and the fact that the Ukraine was a major theater of World War II on the eastern front have meant that all these bureaucracies have been heavily concerned with the Ukraine. In many respects the Ukraine is a microcosm of the U.S.S.R. To be sure, certain problems—such as those arising from invasion and enemy occupation, from expansion of Soviet rule to extensive new territories, and from the persistence of non-Russian national sentiment—are accentuated in the Ukraine. The crises arising from these special problems, however, frequently served to illuminate the basic nature of the Soviet system and, especially, of its political elite.

Even the state and Party bureaucracies which form the Ukrainian apparatus are, of course, not independent. All major policy decisions are made in Moscow. The Ukrainian elite does, however, exercise a considerable range of decision in matters specifically

affecting the region. Since the nearly 41,000,000 people of the
Ukraine comprise one-fifth of the Soviet population, these regional
matters are highly important. In view of the fact that even the
central bureaucratic chiefs were allowed only a limited range of
decision-making during Stalin's lifetime, the still more limited
power of decision of the regional leaders was not qualitatively
different from that of the central elite. An intensive examination
of the elite of the Ukrainian apparatus may, therefore, provide a
significant, though incomplete, guide to the nature of the middle
level of the Soviet elite in general.

Footnotes to Chapter 1

1. Karl Mannheim, *Man and Society in an Age of Reconstruction* (New York: Harcourt, Brace & Co., 1940), p. 75. Cf. Harold D. Lasswell, *Politics: Who Gets What, When, How,* reprinted in *The Political Writings of Harold D. Lasswell* (Glencoe, Ill.: The Free Press, 1951), p. 444.

2. For a detailed analysis, see Barrington Moore, Jr., *Soviet Politics: The Dilemma of Power* (Cambridge, Mass.: Harvard University Press, 1950), especially pp. 64-71 and 228-268; cf. Alex Inkeles, "Social Stratification and Mobility in the Soviet Union: 1940-1950," *American Sociological Review*, XV (August, 1950), 465-479.

3. Joseph Stalin, *Mastering Bolshevism* (New York: Workers Library Publishers, 1937), p. 36, as quoted in Merle Fainsod, *How Russia Is Ruled* (Cambridge, Mass.: Harvard University Press, 1954), p. 178.

4. Vilfredo Pareto, *The Mind and Society,* ed. by Arthur Livingston, trans. by Arthur Livingston and Andrew Bonjorno (New York: Harcourt, Brace & Co., 1935), IV, 1573.

5. M. A. Suslov, Secretary of the Central Committee of the Communist Party of the Soviet Union (CPSU), in his speech to the Twentieth Congress of the CPSU, *Pravda Ukrainy,* February 18, 1956.

6. Cf. Harold D. Lasswell, Daniel Lerner, and C. Easton Rothwell, *The Comparative Study of Elites,* Hoover Institute Studies, Series B: Elites, No. 1 (Stanford: Stanford University Press, 1952), p. 8.

7. "Bureaucracy" in Soviet usage has a negative connotation similar to the frequent popular use of the term in Western countries. While the Soviet institutions here mentioned fit the modern sociological definition of a bureaucracy, it should be noted that they differ from Max Weber's classical model described in "Wirtschaft und Gesellschaft," *Grundriss der Sozialoekonomik,* 3rd. ed. (Tuebingen: J. C. B. Mohr, 1947), pp. 650-678. As there are two excellent critiques of Max Weber's definition, with special reference to the Soviet case, it does not seem necessary to present a detailed discussion of this difference here. See Philip Selznick, "An Approach to a Theory of Bureaucracy," *American Sociological Review*, VIII (February, 1943), 47-54; also see Helen Contas, "Max Weber's Two Conceptions of Bureaucracy," *American Journal of Sociology*, LXIII (January, 1958), 400-409.

8. The "Smolensk archive," which contains not only compiled data but also original documents concerning officials, was captured by the Germans during World War II and is the subject of a study now being completed by Merle Fainsod. This material relates primarily to the pre-Purge period.

9. While it was manifestly impractical to examine all regional newspapers, "spot checks" were made of the following: *Komunist* [Communist], Erivan, Armenian S.S.R.; *Sovetskaia Belorussiia* [Soviet Belorussia], Minsk, Belorussian S.S.R.; *Sovetskaia Kirgiziia* [Soviet Kirgizia], Frunze, Kirgiz S.S.R.; and *Turkmenskaia Iskra* [Turkmen Spark], Ashkhabad, Turkmen S.S.R. Comparative data from these papers will be introduced later in this study.

10. Actually, in order to establish these circumstances and to ensure that earlier information on present officials was not available, Ukrainian materials and the Moscow press (*Vecherniaia Moskva, Pravda, Izvestia*) were examined for all of 1937 and 1938 and, in certain instances, for even earlier periods.

[11.] See Chapter 2, n. 15. For very recent developments affecting some of the highest Ukrainian apparatus officials, see Chapter 10, pp. 146 ff.

[12.] I was able to examine nineteen unpublished dissertations containing material relating to this topic in the Lenin State Library in Moscow during September, 1956, and June, 1958.

[13.] See Khrushchev's secret speech to the Twentieth Congress. (U.S. Department of State version, *The New York Times*, June 5, 1956). As no Ukrainian Republic newspapers are available for the period of German occupation, there are, of course, no reports of Ukrainian Central Committee meetings during that period; probably none were held.

2

The Elite as a Social Group

THE RELATIVE IMPORTANCE of the members of the elite of the Ukrainian apparatus depends primarily on the positions they hold in the bureaucratic structures. Even the more subtle distinctions of influence arising from personal connections of the officials appear to stem indirectly from their careers. The member of the apparatus who exercises influence beyond that conferred by his nominal position is one who usually worked at an earlier stage of his career with, or for, a more powerful official who continues to act as his patron.

Several factors militate against the importance of contacts made outside the official's bureaucratic career. The sheer pressure of duties is such that there is little time for outside activities, except, of course, for the ubiquitous Party indoctrination.[1] For many years the working day for "responsible workers" (i.e., officials of some authority) in the Republic state offices was normally 10 a.m. to 10 p.m., "with an intermission for dinner and earlier closing on Saturdays." This schedule was actually cited as proof that time remained for officials to attend indoctrination courses![2]

One reason why the official's time is so fully occupied is the pressure of his duties. Another reason is his superiors' fear that he might use his spare time to develop interests apart from his Party career. The Communist system frowns upon the development, especially by Party members and officials, of hobbies or avocations. Occasionally, to be sure, we are told that a member of the apparatus pursued some activity which was not directly related to his career. Usually, however, it is some sport which indirectly fitted him for his duties. For example, an obkom (provincial Party committee) secretary in an oblast (province) adjoining the Ukraine is said, approvingly, to have been an ardent hunter and "physical culturist."[3] Conceivably, such an official might make useful contacts among fellow sportsmen, but the opportunities would seem slight. Recent emphasis upon the official's acquiring a rounded cultural background may, however, increase the possibilities of outside contacts of a somewhat different character.

Considerably more important might be the personal relationships arising through family contacts. "It is strictly inconceivable," writes a prominent American sociologist, "that most of the men highly placed in the occupational sphere. . . should not share their prestige [with their families]."[4] In the upper echelons of the central apparatus in Moscow, which are occasionally open to limited observation by foreigners, such contacts would seem to be of some significance in determining elite status. Lack of information on such contacts constitutes perhaps the most important gap in our knowledge concerning the Soviet elite in general.

The "iron curtain" which hides families from public notice is, of course, the creation of Communist policy. One of the most consistent themes of Communist ideology has been the primacy of societal over personal interests. Family connections, while accepted as essential, must always remain subordinate to service to the Party and the state. The "proper" attitude is well expressed in the memoirs of Aleksei Fedorovich Fedorov, the first secretary of Chernigov obkom. When he arrived home from an exhausting official trip, his wife's first words were: "At last! A man's been calling you all morning." As it turned out the matter was really important, for Fedorov's subordinate wished to inform him of the outbreak of war. From then on, Fedorov's family was left to its own devices:

> Days passed without my seeing my wife and children.
> I could not manage to be with my family even on the day they left Chernigov. I arrived at the station a bare minute before the train left, and it started to pull out in the middle of my parting words to my wife and children.[5]

While, in recent years, family members of a few prominent Soviet leaders have appeared at semi-official gatherings— perhaps to prove to the outside world that the leaders are really human— even the death of Stalin did not lead to any marked relaxation of the rule that personal attachments are not matters of public interest.

The Soviet system provides several categories which indicate the importance of officials in the apparatus. The broadest category is that of "directing cadres". A single oblast may have 1,000 officials in this group, and the total for the Ukraine probably exceeds 50,000.[6] While these officials may be considered part of the elite— i.e., to use Stalin's term, the "non-commissioned officers"—they are too numerous, and data on individual members are too scarce to permit detailed analysis.

At the other extreme is the Ukrainian Party Presidium, known until September, 1952, as the Politburo. This body has varied in number from eight (in 1938) to thirteen (in 1952); it now totals ten members, including candidate members. Typically, the Presidium has included three or four of the most important secretaries of the Central Committee; the Chairman of the Presidium of the Supreme Soviet; the Chairman of the Council of Ministers and two or three of his deputies; and the Commanding General of the Kiev Military District. Before the war the director of the NKVD was a member, and occasionally first secretaries of the most important obkoms are members. All of these, however, are really among the upper, rather than the middle, level of the elite, as is evidenced by the fact that they are usually elected to membership in the Central Committee of the CPSU. Because of the key role of these leaders in the Ukrainian apparatus, many of their careers will be analyzed individually in connection with the branches of the apparatus which they have controlled.

At the oblast level the obkom bureaus correspond to the Central Committee Presidium. In many respects membership in the bureaus is an excellent criterion of middle-level elite status. The comparatively few records available indicate that a fairly uniform pattern is followed in appointing the bureaus. In addition to the four or five obkom secretaries, who are always members, the bureau includes the chairman of the oblast executive committee (head of the state apparatus), the secretary of the Party committee of the chief city of the oblast, the editor of the principal newspaper, the first secretary of the Komsomol organization, and the director of the oblast police apparatus. A very large bureau may include such other officials as state or industrial directors and military officers. In effect, the obkom bureau is a standing committee of the heads of the most important branches of the apparatus in the province.

The obkom bureaus contain a large proportion of the middle-level elite, but they do not, of course, embrace the large number of officials of this category in the Kiev headquarters of the various branches of the Ukrainian apparatus. The Congresses of the KPU and the Central Committee, on the other hand, include both Republic and oblast officials. Consequently, while they include some persons of little political importance, these bodies afford a more comprehensive index of the middle-level elite. Of still greater practical importance, information on their composition is much more complete. While lists of obkom bureau members appear only sporadically, the complete Central Committee membership is published after each Party Congress. Lists of delegates to the Party Congresses themselves are not available, but the Soviet sources do publish considerable statistical material on the delegates' backgrounds.

TABLE 1

APPARATUS LEVELS REPRESENTED AT CONGRESSES
OF THE K.P.U.[7]

(Percentages)

	1949	1952	1954
Republic organizations	10.7	8.1	9.0
Oblast organizations	26.6	20.1	19.1
City and raion (county) organizations	30.5	32.6	36.2
Manufacturing and transportation	13.3	15.3	11.7
Collective farms, MTS, sovkhozes	7.3	7.9	10.5
Educational institutions	2.1	4.8	3.4
Other	9.5	11.2	10.0

Delegates to the Ukrainian Party Congress have averaged about 700 in number, while KPU Central Committee membership (including candidate members) has always been below 200. The

Central Committee, therefore, is a considerably more select group. Nevertheless, the two bodies are roughly comparable as segments of the elite. Since a number of the characteristics of the Central Committee membership can be calculated independently, the Soviet data concerning the backgrounds of Congress delegates are subject to control.[8]

TABLE 2

POSITIONS REPRESENTED IN CONGRESS AND CENTRAL COMMITTEES OF THE K.P.U.

(Reported percentages of Congress delegates; calculated percentages of *identified* Central Committee members and candidates *only*.)

Type of Apparatus Position	1938		1940		1949		1952		1954		1956	
	Cong.	CC	Cong.	CC	Cong.	CC	Cong.	CC	Cong.	CC	Cong.	CC
Party	–	49	52	39	47	46	44	49	46	42	46	42
State and Trade Union	–	22	13	40	13	27	13	25	13	37	13	35
Army and MVD	–	7	17	6	13	8	16	4	12	6	11	5
Komsomol	–	–	–	1	–	1	2	1	2	1	2	1
Industry and Transportation	–	14	14	10	14	13	14	13	12	6	14	8
Agriculture (low level only)	–	7	3	4	8	4	8	4	8	2	11	2
Cultural Institutions	–	–	2	–	4	2	5	4	7	2	4	4
Percentages of CC Identified		49		69		76		61		58		68
Women*	–	4	–	2	10	4	13	7	13	5	14	5

* All women identified as such in the Central Committee are given here as a percentage of the total of Central Committee members and candidates (in Russian and Ukrainian a name can always be identified as that of a man or a woman if the patronymic is known; Russian last names can usually be identified by sex, but Ukrainian often cannot; hence there is no assurance that all women have been identified). A breakdown of positions held by women in the 1954 Congress delegation indicates that most were in low-level agricultural positions; in fact, women constituted a majority of the delegates from agriculture.

Perhaps the most interesting information available on the background of the Ukrainian Party Congress members is that relating to their nationality, for such data have not been published for any considerable group of officials of the Soviet Union as a whole for more than two decades. Moreover, reports of Party Congresses in the other Union Republics apparently rarely contain information on the nationalities of the delegates.[9]

TABLE 3

NATIONALITY OF DELEGATES TO K.P.U. CONGRESSES

	1940	1949	1952	1954	1956
Ukrainian	55.4	60.9	66.2	65.0	67.8
Russian	37.6	35.6	30.9	33.0	29.6
Jewish	4.1	–	–	–	–
Other	2.9	3.5	2.9	2.0	2.6

That the Ukrainian Party should find it desirable to publish such statistics concerning its bureaucracy is remarkable, in view of the fact that the "proper" attitude of an official is usually to regard nationality as a matter of complete indifference. An anecdote related by Fedorov, the obkom secretary quoted earlier, illustrates this attitude:

> There was only one person who tried to steer an underhanded course. . . "And may I ask whether you're Ukrainian?" "What's the point?" I rejoined, on my guard. "Nothing special . . . Your name's Fyodorov, but you look like one of us . . . " "I'm Russian," I said (although actually I consider myself Ukrainian). "Does that make any difference?"[10]

It would appear likely that the publication of the statistics of delegates' nationalities is mainly intended to impress the Ukrainian population that its group has a majority among Party officials, and that this majority is slowly but steadily increasing. An unpublished Soviet source, based on the archives of the Section of Party Organs of the Central Committee of the KPU, states that on January 1, 1951, Ukrainians comprised 71.4 per cent of the "directing cadres"—a much greater proportion, though for a considerably lower category of officials, than that indicated for the Congress delegations.[11] Consequently, there seems no reason to doubt the validity of the nationality statistics published at the time of the Congresses. At the same time, it should be noted that Russians are at least fifty per cent more heavily represented in the Congresses than in the general population of the Republic. According to Soviet sources, the population is now seventy-five per cent Ukrainian; consequently, assuming the continued presence of small Jewish and Polish minorities, the Russian element could scarcely exceed twenty per cent.[12]

In 1940, on the other hand, only sixty-three per cent of the total number of Communists in the Ukraine were Ukrainians, while 19.1 per cent were Russian and 13.4 per cent were Jewish.[13] Probably the large turnover in membership during and immediately after the war increased the proportion of Ukrainians considerably. It seems, however, that there is a constant decline in the proportion of Ukrainians as one proceeds from the population at large toward the elite strata. One reason for this situation is the influx of Russian officials from outside the Ukraine. The Ukrainian apparatus at the lower levels is by no means a closed group; it is subject to considerable interchange of personnel with other branches of the Party and state bureaucracies. This apparently was especially the case immediately after World War II, when the apparatus was heavily depleted; on April 20, 1944, 2,965 persons were sent from the "eastern oblasts of the U.S.S.R." to take posts in the Ukraine. Up to 1946, 800 had been dispatched to posts in Vinnitsa oblast alone.[14] Apparently, however, there is much less interchange of higher officials between the Ukrainian and other apparatuses.[15] Of twenty-six such officials for whom place of birth has been reported, twenty were born in the Ukraine. It seems, therefore, that most of the Russians in the higher levels of the Ukrainian apparatus elite are natives of the Ukraine or that they went there at an early stage of their careers.

It appears likely that Ukrainians are relatively more weakly represented in the apparatus than are Russians because the former are largely of peasant background, while Communists have been predominantly urban intellectuals and laborers by origin. It is also possible, though not demonstrable, that Ukrainians have been deliberately discriminated against because they are suspected of being inclined to nationalist opposition to the regime. Possibly, too, the Ukrainians themselves have not been attracted by Party service.

The position in the elite of the third most numerous group of the Ukraine's population, the Jews, is puzzling. Before the war (but after the annexation of territories acquired from Poland and Rumania) Jews comprised about five per cent of the population of the Ukrainian S.S.R. Their proportion in the 1940 Congress delegation is not much short of that figure. It is, however, considerably below the 13.4 per cent of Jews in the Party membership. Jews, moreover, were much more heavily represented in the population of the larger cities, where Party activities centered. In the 1940 city Party congress in Kiev, Jews comprised 25.4 per cent of the delegates—probably about the same proportion as the Jewish element in the population of Kiev.[16]

It would seem that Jews were deliberately restricted to a lower proportion of the higher and more conspicuous levels of Party leadership. Probably there was a desire to avoid arousing the latent anti-Semitic feelings of the population against the regime. In addition, Jews may have been regarded with suspicion by Stalin and his associates because a large number of the purged Party leaders were Jewish. It is also likely, of course, that many persons of Jewish background listed themselves as Russian or Ukrainian to avoid either popular or official disfavor.[17] After the war the category of Jews was dropped entirely in analyses of Congress membership; the fact that the residual "other" category was not significantly enlarged indicates that indentifiable Jews occupied a still smaller place in the elite. This may have been in part due to the elimination of a large portion of the Jews in the Ukraine through evacuation and through the Nazi extermination policy; to some extent it appears to have been the result of a planned, but limited, policy of discrimination.

Perhaps the background factor most likely to be distorted in Soviet statistics is "social origin"—i. e., the occupation of one's father. The regime desires to convey the impression that its officials are predominantly lower-class; the officials themselves find it desirable to indicate that they are of "exploited" rather than "exploiter" origin. Generally speaking, statistics on this subject have not been published since the war. In 1938 Khrushchev, apparently referring to social origin rather than present occupation, stated that seventy-one per cent of the Party members and candidate members were workers, twenty-one per cent were peasants, and seven and one-half per cent were employees (i. e., white-collar workers).[18] It is important to note, too, that about one-third of the biographical statements, which might be expected to refer to this point, omit it. Of the remaining twenty-three, fourteen indicate the official came from a peasant family, with the qualification "poor" or "tenant" usually added. Only eight uniformly indicate working-class origin. The numbers involved are too small to be of great significance, but it is perhaps surprising that such a large proportion should indicate peasant, rather than worker, background.

In addition to throwing light on the nationality and social background of elite members, the data reported for Congress delegations help greatly in determining the rate of turnover of officials in the apparatus.

TABLE 4

PERIODS DURING WHICH DELEGATES TO CONGRESSES OF THE K.P.U. HAD BECOME PARTY MEMBERS*

Period	1938 Cong. No.	%	1949 Cong. No.	%	1952 Con. No.	%	1954 Cong. No.	%	1956 Cong. No.	%
Before 1917	12	2.1	7	1.0	6	.8	6	.7	5	.6
1917 - 1920	110	19.4	38	5.8	25	3.3	25	2.8	19	2.2
1921 - 1930	361	63.3	325	49.5	277	35.9	267	30.1	204	23.6
1931 - 1940	86	15.2	201	30.6	290	37.6	338	38.2	330	38.1
1941 - date of Congress	–	–	86	13.1	173	22.4	250	28.2	308	35.6

*In some instances, Soviet statistics contain breakdowns for shorter periods; the figures have been combined in this table in order to make data for all Congresses comparable.

The data on the periods at which Congress delegates entered the Party, presented in Table 4, are closely related to the question

of turnover. Individual delegates may, of course, have been replaced at succeeding Congresses by others who entered the Party
during the same period. Nevertheless, decreases in the absolute
numbers of delegates who entered the Party during the same period
indicate minimum rates of turnover.

Since the Great Purge, the number of pre-1917 entrants, i. e.,
of the "Old Bolsheviks," has been a very small one, and normal
deaths could easily account for its slow, absolute decline. The
"Revolutionary" and "Civil War" Communists (who entered
1917-1920) present almost the same picture in the Congress delegations from 1949 on; at the 1938 Congress, on the other hand,
they formed a sizeable minority. While no statistics on the dates of
delegates' entry into the Party were provided at the Fifteenth
Ukrainian Congress (1940), some revealing data can be obtained
from the record of the Eighteenth All-Union Congress (in 1939),
which contains the date of Party entry of each delegate. Forty-
four of the Eighteenth Congress delegates were included in the
Ukrainian Central Committee in 1938, in 1940, or in both years.
Of these, thirteen—or about thirty per cent—entered the Party
in the period 1917-1920. Only five of these officials appear to have
survived World War II in high positions.[19] This fact, together
with the drastic decline in the proportion of 1917-1920 entrants
at the 1949 Congress, seems to indicate that World War II was
especially hard upon the Communists of Revolutionary and Civil
War origin.

The groups of Party entrants discussed in the preceding paragraph became Party members before Stalin had assumed the
post of General Secretary. Most of the group entering between
1921 and 1930, on the other hand, became members while he was
consolidating control of the Party machinery. Moreover, available
biographical information indicates that most of those who entered
the Party during the twenties began their careers as apparatus
officials after Stalin's control of the machine was complete. They
came under the influence of the dictator and his associates during
their formative years in the Party. Very probably many of them
became "his men." As Table 4 shows, these men have continued
to form a remarkably stable group among Congress delegates.

Their absolute numbers have declined by about two-fifths, a rather small rate of attrition for a span of eighteen years. An examination of available biographical information concerning prominent Party officials also indicates that entrants during the twenties have been markedly successful in attaining and holding elite position. If one excludes several very high officials, such as Khrushchev, who tend to be older and who therefore entered the Party before 1921, the preponderance of 1921-1930 entrants is overwhelming.

The great absolute and relative increase of delegates who entered the Party after 1931 indicates that the Party elite is open—at the bottom—to new blood. All available evidence indicates, however, that persons who entered the Party after 1930, although they are plentiful in the lower reaches of the apparatus, have not as yet reached the "middle level" of the elite in large numbers.

TABLE 5

AGES OF DELEGATES TO K.P.U. CONGRESSES

	1949 Cong.		1952 Cong.		1954 Cong.		1956 Cong.	
	No.	%	No.	%	No.	%	No.	%
Age Group								
Under 35	41	6.2	60	7.8	103	11.5	76	8.8
36 - 40	134	20.4	128	16.7	138	15.5	139	16.1
41 - 50	415	63.1	476	61.7	520	58.3	489	56.5
Over 50	67	10.2	107	13.8	131	14.7	162	18.7

The conclusions concerning the role of the 1921-1930 Party entrants are borne out by an examination of the age structure of the Ukrainian apparatus elite. The most striking feature of the data presented in Table 5 is the appreciable relative increase—and the rapid absolute increase—of delegates over fifty years old. In the relatively short span of seven years, the number in this category increased by nearly one hundred.

An examination of biographical data on this subject is somewhat unsatisfactory, since most material has to be drawn from obituaries, which would naturally tend to relate to the older men. It is all the more significant, therefore, that of the thirty-eight relatively important Party officials for whom such information is available, twenty-five were born between 1901 and 1908. All of this group were, of course, between forty-one and fifty years old in 1949, and nearly all were over fifty in 1956. Only in rare instances had a member of this group joined the Party before 1921 (when the oldest was twenty), but most had joined by 1930.[20] Both age distribution and period of Party entrance point to the existence of a relatively stable elite group, who were born between 1900 and 1907 and who entered the Party during the years when Stalin was overcoming his rivals. While evidence on this point is not conclusive, it seems that this group has held the most important apparatus posts from the time of the end of the Great Purge to the present. Lower Party officials, on the other hand, are predominantly younger, with no definite tendency toward a relative increase of the older age groups.

TABLE 6

AGES OF "DIRECTING CADRES" IN THE UKRAINE

Age Group	January 1, 1951 (percentages)	January 1, 1955 (percentages)
Under 30	19	10.9
31-35	19	26.9
Total under 35	38	37.8
36-40	21.5	22.2
41-45	18.4	18.6
46-50	15	12.2
Total 41-50	33.4	30.8
Over 50	7.1	9.2

Since such a high proportion of the members of the present elite were in their thirties when they were called to major posts during the Great Purge—and since these members are still for the most part under fifty-five—losses through natural deaths have apparently been relatively small. While a considerable number may have died without public notice, the very small number of obituaries of middle-level officials is noticeable, averaging about two a year.

It may be expected, however, that the number of deaths in the elite of the apparatus will soon show a marked upturn. The Party and state officials in high office—especially those who attained important posts during the Great Purge and went through the war in responsible positions—have been subjected to enormous psychological and physical strains. As indicated earlier, even the "normal" working schedule has imposed a very heavy burden upon them. At times of crisis, they are not encouraged to coddle themselves. Describing the difficulties of the efforts of Party officials to escape German capture, Fedorov relates a conversation with the first secretary of the Zhitomir oblast committee:

> Big, flabby Syromyatnikov mentioned his heart: it was beating irregularly, he said.
> I tried to cheer him up. "Now what's a little thing like that? Just don't pay any attention to your heart, Comrade Syromyatnikov. And, in general, remember that the heart is a civilian organ; best to leave it behind when you go to war,
> Thus I jollied Syromyatnikov along, but I must admit I was glad to second him when he asked for a halt: he was having difficulty in breathing.[21]

Apparently Siromiatnikov did not survive this ordeal, for he has never been mentioned since the war.

Occasionally, there is evidence that even the apparently fit fail to hold up under the strain of life in the apparatus. The "physical culturist and ardent hunter" mentioned earlier in this chapter is a case in point:

> He was still young, but he had borne on his shoulders the stages of Komsomol, Party, and Chekist [police] work; he did not lose his self-possession, although he had to strain his will and his intellect to the utmost in the new circumstances of the war by taking on an extra burden of work to compensate for his in-

sufficient experience. . . . Matveev was a trained director,
a man of the Stalinist governing school and of Stalinist temper
. . . . He was broad-shouldered, muscular, and wore a
leather jacket which admirably set off his well-proportioned
figure. . . . Not only did he never have a toothache, but it
appeared that no human ailment ever afflicted this healthy,
cheerful fellow. Shortly after the war he suddenly died of a
heart attack. Evidently his heart could not stand the heavy
strain.[22]

The change of the composition of the Congress delegations provides a revealing, though indirect, index to the rate of turnover
in the elite. A more precise indication is furnished by an actual
comparison of the lists of persons elected to the Central Committee
at succeeding Congresses.

TABLE 7

PROPORTION OF NEWLY-ELECTED MEMBERS AND
CANDIDATE MEMBERS IN THE CENTRAL
COMMITTEE OF THE K.P.U.

Year of Election of Central Committee	Total Number (Mem. and Cand.)	Number Elected for First Time	% Elected for First Time
1938	86	84	98
1940	119	73	62
1949	123	93	76
1952	160	87	54
1954	173	48	28
1956	173	52	30

The data presented in Table 7 indicate that after each Congress
the Central Committee contains a very high proportion of "new
blood." A cursory examination of the data would also suggest
that there has been a decline in the rate of turnover of the elite
as represented by the Central Committee members and candidate
members. Actually, this trend is only apparent, arising from the
fluctuations in the size of the Central Committee and the very
great differences in intervals between elections. The analysis presented in Table 8 indicates that, taking account of these factors,
the elimination of members and candidates from the Central Committee has proceeded at a fairly even rate of about twenty per cent

per year. The only exception is the interval between 1940 and 1949, when the "rate of attrition" was only nine per cent per year.

TABLE 8

RATE OF ATTRITION OF MEMBERS AND CANDIDATE MEMBERS OF THE CENTRAL COMMITTEE OF THE K.P.U.

Time of Initial Election to CC*	Number in Group	Number Not Continuing in CC at Following Election	Interval Between Elections (Years)	Average Attrition Per Year	Average Annual Attrition as % of Number in Groups
June, 1938	84	39	1.9	20	24
May, 1940	73	62	8.6	7	9
January, 1949	93	47	2.7	17	19
September, 1952	87	23	1.5	15	16
March, 1954	47	20	1.9	11	23
January, 1956	53	—	—	—	—

*The "time of initial election" refers to the time at which the individual is first reported to be elected. Elections to the Central Committee are made only by the Congresses. An individual may, however, be "co-opted" to the Central Committee; considerable evidence indicates that this does, in fact, take place whenever an official receives a post high enough to warrant his entry into this body. Consequently, a number of individuals in each group were actually members or candidates before the date of election shown.

The explanation for the apparent longevity of the 1940 group seems to be that a high proportion of those elected to the Central Committee at any given time are removed from it within a few years, while those who survive this initial period have a good chance of remaining in the Central Committee almost indefinitely.

The data presented in Table 9 suggest that about half of each newly-elected group of Central Committee members and candidates tends to be eliminated within two or three years. While the multitude of complicating factors and the small number of groups which were elected sufficiently long ago to permit extended observation make no further generalization fully demonstrable, it seems that the process of attrition becomes markedly slower after the elimination of this initial group. Indeed, the small contingents

TABLE 9

MEMBERS AND CANDIDATE MEMBERS OF THE
CENTRAL COMMITTEE OF THE K.P.U.
REELECTED AT SUCCESSIVE CONGRESSES

Year of Initial Election	Number in Group	1938	1940	Reelected 1949	1952	1954	1956
1937 or earlier	—	2	1	1	—	—	—
1938	84	—	45	18	16	13	11
1940	73	—	—	11	10	9	7
1949	93	—	—	—	47	40	31
1952	87	—	—	—	—	64	46
1954	47	—	—	—	—	—	28
1956	53	—	—	—	—	—	—

of the first two groups elected after the Great Purge who remained in the Central Committee until 1949 seem to have a good prospect of indefinite membership, for several of the subsequent eliminations from the groups can be explained by deaths or transfers outside the Ukraine.

While one can assume that there are many hidden factors influencing membership in the Ukrainian elite, the available evidence indicates that the primary criterion is position in the apparatus. About half of the elite members are Party officials, while most of the remainder are officials in the state bureaucracy.

Ukrainians by nationality appear to comprise a majority of the officials, but Russians are represented disproportionately to their numbers in the general population. The great majority of the elite members are certainly of obscure birth; the danger of bias in available data makes it difficult to determine whether most really sprang from peasant and worker stock, but on the whole this seems probable.

Turnover in the elite is sufficiently rapid, especially at the bottom, to provide ample opportunity for new talent. Nevertheless, since 1938 the center of gravity of the power structure has apparently remained in the group of men who were given power as a result of the Great Purge. Despite the excessive strains to which Communist leadership is subject, the "men of '38," now in their early fifties, are at the prime of their power, and they may be expected to remain dominant for another decade. During the middle years of the 1960's, however, one may anticipate that a large portion of this group will die or become incapacitated. They will be replaced by men who came to posts of responsibility during or after the war. These men, to be sure, grew up under Stalin and even began their careers in higher posts while he was still alive. Most did not, however, endure the terrible and morally corrupting experience to which officials in important posts were subjected during the thirties. These circumstances make the process by which new leaders are formed of crucial importance.

Footnotes to Chapter 2

[1] Since Party organizations are formed in places of employment, however, Party activity is really an aspect of the official's duties.

[2] Mariia Maksimovna Pidtychenko, Secretary of Propaganda for Kiev city Party committee, "Ob ideinom urovne rukovodiashchikh sovetskikh kadrov [Concerning the Level of Ideas of Directing Soviet Cadres], *Pravda Ukrainy* (hereafter cited as *PU*), August 30, 1945. Apparently the extremely late hours, established to conform to Stalin's own peculiar working habits, have been abandoned since his death.

[3] Peter Vershigora, *Liudi s chistoi sovest'iu* [People With Clean Consciences] (Moscow: Sovetskii Pisatel', rev. ed., 1951), p. 49.

[4] Talcott Parsons, *The Social System* (Glencoe, Illinois: The Free Press, 1951), pp. 160-161 (quoted by permission).

[5] Aleksei Fedorovich Fedorov,, *The Underground Committee Carries On* (Moscow: Foreign Languages Publishing House, 1952), pp. 11-13. This is a translation of the first part of Fedorov's memoirs (published in Russian in 1947).

[6] On January 1, 1955, Drogobych oblast had over 1,000 "directing workers"; L'vov oblast had 913 on January 1, 1951. See I. T. Pinegin, "Rabota KP Ukrainy po osushchestvleniiu reshenii partii o podbore, rasstanovke i vospitanii rukovodiashchikh partiinykh i sovetskikh kadrov v poslevoennyi period (1946-1955 gg.)" [The Work of the Communist Party of the Ukraine in Carrying Out the Decision of the Party Concerning the Selection, Assignment, and Training of Directing Party and Soviet Cadres in the Postwar Period (1946-1955)], an unpublished dissertation for obtaining the academic degree of candidate of historical sciences in the Academy of Social Sciences of the Central Committee of the CPSU, Moscow, 1955, p. 174. Table 6 below is based on this source, p. 111.

[7] All data for composition of Congress membership in this and other tables in this chapter are based on figures provided in the reports of the Credentials Committee of the Congresses. Sources for the Congresses are as follows: Fourteenth Congress (June, 1938), *Visti*, June 17, 1938; Fifteenth Congress (May, 1940), *Kolhospnyk Ukraïny*, May 17, 1940; Sixteenth Congress (January, 1949), *PU*, February 5, 1949; Seventeenth Congress (September, 1952), *PU*, September 26, 1952; Eighteenth Congress (March, 1954), *Radians'ka Ukraïna* (hereafter cited as *RU*), March 26, 1954; Nineteenth Congress (January, 1956), *PU*, January 20, 1956. Data in all categories are not, of course, available for all Congresses. Data presented apply to full delegates only; the relatively small number of delegates "with consultative votes" has not been included.

[8] While independently calculated, the distribution of Central Committee membership is, of course, ultimately derived from Soviet sources. The process involves the identification of persons listed as elected to the Central Committee by finding them listed elsewhere as holding specific positions in the apparatus, at a time or under circumstances which make it probable that they held the same post when elected to the Central Committee. It seems most unlikely that the Soviet press could afford in any considerable number of cases to list a high- or medium-rank official as holding a position which he did not in fact hold.

[9] Of those checked at random, only the Fifth (1949) and Sixth (1952) Congresses of the Kirgiz Party revealed the delegates' nationalities. Neither

of the accounts of the Armenian Party Congresses (Fourteenth [1948] and Sixteenth [1952]) which I examined included the reports of the Credentials Committee, which presumably contained this information, though the report of the Fourteenth Congress (*Komunist* [Erivan], November 13, 1948) noted that a Credentials Committee report was delivered. Reports of the Nineteenth (1949) and Twentieth (1952) Congresses of the Belorussian Party and of the Eleventh Congress of the Turkmen Party (1952) are also devoid of nationality data.

10. Fedorov, p. 27. This does not prevent Soviet Ukrainian publications from printing blatant appeals to national sentiments (see John A. Armstrong, *Ukrainian Nationalism, 1939-1945* [New York: Columbia University Press, 1955], p. 176).

11. Pinegin, p. 111. A published source states, however, that on January 1, 1956, the proportion of Ukrainians among "directing workers" of the KPU was 68.8 per cent. See I. Kravtsev, "Leninskaia natsional'naia politika i ee osushchestylenie na Ukraine" [Leninist National Policy and Its Realization in the Ukraine], *PU*, December 25, 1956.

12. N. I. Lialikov, *Sovetskaia Ukraina: ocherk ekonomicheskoi geografii* [The Soviet Ukraine: A Sketch of Economic Geography] (Moscow: Gosudarstvennoe Izdatel'stvo Geograficheskoi Literatury, 1954), p. 90. I would guess that this is considerably underestimated. As early as 1937, eighty-two per cent of the school children of the Ukraine were in Ukrainian-language schools. The West Ukrainian areas annexed later were overwhelmingly Ukrainian ethnically,

13. Khrushchev's speech to the Fifteenth Congress, *Kolhospnyk Ukraïny*, May 20, 1940.

14. V. I. Zhadovets, "Deiatel'nost' kommunisticheskoi partii v oblasti dal'-neishego ukrepleniia sovetskogo gosudarstvennogo apparata v gody chet-vertoi piatiletki (na materialiakh Ukrainskoi S.S.R.)" [The Activity of the Communist Party in the Area of Further Strengthening the Soviet State Apparatus During the Years of the Fourth Five-Year Plan (From Materials of the Ukrainian S.S.R.)], an unpublished dissertation for obtaining the academic degree of candidate of historical sciences in the Institute for Improving the Qualifications of Teachers of Marxism-Leninism, Kiev University, 1956, p. 215.

15. In order to gather all the available evidence on transfers of officials into and out of the Ukrainian apparatus, one would have to trace the careers of all officials throughout the U.S.S.R. for at least the past twenty years. Such an undertaking would have been impossible within the limits of a case study. Moreover, the comparative lack of reporting of names of officials for areas outside the Ukraine would have made even the most exhaustive process of tracing unsatisfactory. Consequently, the effort to determine outside transfers or origins of officials of the Ukrainian apparatus has been limited to what may be described as "spot checking." *Pravda*, the principal Party paper in the U.S.S.R., for the period from January, 1937, through March, 1956, has been checked against a name file of Ukrainian officials. In addition, certain other non-Ukrainian newspaper sources have been checked for specific periods. These include *Izvestia* (Moscow) for 1937-44; *Krasnaia Bashkiriia* (scattered numbers for 1943); *Krasnaia Zvezda* (September-December, 1939; June-July, 1940); and the compilation of lists of Republic Central Committees (originally published in the Republic newspapers) published in *Current Digest of the Soviet Press*, 1956.

16. *Visti*, March 6, 1940.

[17.] Nationality identification in the U.S.S.R. is essentially a matter of personal choice, but it is formally registered on each individual's identification card.

[18.] *Visti*, June 16, 1938. Cf. Chapter 7.

[19.] Of the five, most were men like Khrushchev and Marshal Timoshenko, whose prominence was probably sufficient to protect them from elimination for initial blunders in the conduct of the war, and who were certainly spared most of the physical dangers arising from hostilities.

[20.] Actually, two of the group are stated to have joined the Party while in their teens, before 1921. A few biographies of middle-level officials in Central Asia suggest that the age level is lower and the length of Party membership is shorter there than in the Ukraine. This is probably attributable to the relatively late period in which Communist authority became fully established among the Moslems.

[21.] Fedorov, p. 46.

[22.] Vershigora, p. 49.

3

Training for Rule

AFTER THE GREAT PURGE the Party apparatus still consisted overwhelmingly of men of humble backgrounds and restricted education. In early 1939 only forty per cent of the raikom (county Party committee) and gorkom (city Party committee) secretaries had completed their secondary education; an even smaller proportion (eighteen of forty-eight) of the obkom secretaries had attained this level. Even at that date, however, sixty-five per cent of the obkom section directors—officials with more specialized duties—had completed their secondary schooling.[1]

This situation was a cause for serious dissatisfaction among the Party leaders, for new personnel with so little education could scarcely operate the complex apparatus which the Purge had deprived of experienced officials. As a result the Party made strenuous efforts to raise the level of education of its officials. At the same time a larger proportion of the apparatus officials was drawn from the better educated. By mid-1940, after new elections had replaced many of the 1939 group, 56.6 per cent of the raikom secretaries had secondary educations.[2]

After the war the level of education in the Party rose rapidly, until in 1949 almost twice as large a proportion of Communists (35.2 per cent) had completed secondary educations as was the case in 1939.[3] As Table 10 shows, the level of education in the elite, as represented by the Congress delegates, rose even more rapidly. As early as 1949 about eighty-five per cent had completed secondary educations. This was apparently the "saturation" point, the small remaining minority consisting of peasants and others chosen as figureheads and, perhaps, of a few old Party officials who were unable to correct their early educational deficiencies. Significantly, however, while the number of those with

TABLE 10

EDUCATION OF DELEGATES TO K.P.U. CONGRESSES*

Year of Congress	Higher or Incomplete Higher Education		Secondary Education		Elementary or Incomplete Secondary Education	
	No.	%	No.	%	No.	%
1938	115	20.2	169	29.8	285	50.0
1940	161	28.2	207	36.3	206	35.5
1949	311	47.4	244	37.1	102	15.5
1952	459	59.5	197	25.5	115	14.9
1954	640	71.7	149	16.7	103	11.6
1956	604	70.0	135	16.0	127	14.0

* For the sources of this data, see p. 28 above.

inferior educations remained constant from 1949 on, the number of those who had attained some higher education continued to rise rapidly. The same tendencies, though at a slower rate, are observable among the lower categories of officials, as indicated in Table 11.

TABLE 11

EDUCATION OF "DIRECTING CADRES" IN THE UKRAINE*

Date	Higher Education	Incomplete Higher Education	Specialized Secondary Education	General Secondary Education	Incomplete Secondary Education	Elementary Education
January 1, 1951	21	16.5	15.4	21.5	18.5	7.1
January 1, 1955	34.2	22.2	16.1	13	12.1	2.4

* I. T. Pinegin, "Rabota KP Ukrainy po osushchestvleniiu reshenii partii o podbore, rasstanovke i vospitanii rukovodiashchikh partiinykh i sovetskikh kadrov v poslevoennyi period (1946-1955 gg.)" [The Work of the Communist Party of the Ukraine in Carrying Out the Decisions of the Party Concerning the Selection, Assignment, and Training of Directing Party and Soviet Cadres in the Postwar Period (1946-1955)], an unpublished dissertation for obtaining the academic degree of candidate of historical sciences in the Academy of Social Sciences of the Central Committee of the CPSU, Moscow, 1955, p. 111.

The Party has placed enormous emphasis on increased education, not only because it directly improves the official's job performance but because it prepares him to cope with the problems of an increasingly complex society and to deal with the growing number of well-educated persons in the general population:

> Daily study, ceaseless increase of knowledge, expansion of one's mental outlook—these are vitally indispensable for every Party worker. In his practical activity he will have occasion to encounter the most varied questions. People working in diverse aspects of economic and cultural development will approach him. The director of the enterprise and the chairman of the kolkhoz will await his counsel and assistance. Practitioners of science, workers in literature and art will listen to him. Workers and kolkhozniks will go to him. He will be called to direct skillfully not only individual persons, but entire collectives. He will have to acquaint himself with manufacturing and agriculture, finances and trade, theaters and schools. In a word, there are no questions which might not interest a Party worker. It is understandable that he can correctly decide all these questions only if he has studied affairs deeply.[4]

To a considerable degree the increased educational level of Party and state officials is the result of intensive training courses in Party schools. While practically all officials attend numerous seminars and part-time Party courses such as those given at the "Evening Universities of Marxism-Leninism" in the major cities, the more promising are selected for periods of fulltime training in Party schools especially designed for members of the apparatus. In the Ukraine, until World War II, the Party schools functioned at the obkom level and were especially concerned with training the subordinate officials of the lower Party organizations. In 1938 the Party schools enrolled 363 second and third secretaries of gorkoms and raikoms, 800 instructors of such committees, and 6,631 secretaries of primary organizations.[5] Shortly after the close of the war the Central Committee of the VKP(b) provided for the establishment of regular two-year oblast Party schools in Kharkov, Odessa, Dnepropetrovsk, Stalino, and L'vov.[6] By 1952 the L'vov school alone had graduated 296 directing officials.[7]

Somewhat later these institutions were officially redesignated "inter-oblast" schools and the full term of the course was lengthened to four years.[8] A large proportion of the higher officials of the raikoms take the longer courses. The inter-oblast schools continued, however, to prepare a large proportion of the lower level of apparatus personnel—secretaries of primary Party organizations and village soviets—in part-time courses six months long.[9]

While the minor officials of the apparatus receive their Party training at the obkom level, those who have attained, or are close to attaining, major posts receive more advanced instruction. The principal institutions for such training are the Higher Party School of the Central Committee of the CPSU in Moscow and the Higher Party School of the Central Committee of the Communist Party of the Ukraine in Kiev, usually known as the Republic Higher Party School.

At the present time the Ukrainian Higher School, unlike those of the other Union Republics, offers training of the same quality as that offered in Moscow; both provide four-year programs of "university-level" instruction. Nevertheless, a Ukrainian correspondence section of the CPSU school, formed in 1944, continues to provide training for many important Ukrainian Party and state officials.[10]

An approximate division of apparatus students among the various types of schools is indicated by the report that during 1948-1950 the L'vov obkom assigned twenty-two to the Correspondence section of the Higher Party School of the CPSU, forty to the Republic Higher Party School, and 113 to the oblast school.[11]

The Republic School has attained its present status gradually. It began in September, 1944, as a one-year Party School of the Central Committee of the KP(b)U. In the autumn of 1946 it received its present designation, and the complete course was lengthened to two years. Several years later the term was increased to three, then to four years.[12]

Since its inception the Republic Higher Party School, like other Party training institutions, has been supervised by the agitation and propaganda arm of the Party. The 1946 appointment as its director of Andrei Terenteiovich Chekaniuk, former Deputy Director of the Propaganda and Agitation Administration of the Central Committee, emphasized this link. Nevertheless, the Higher Party School has maintained a close association with non-Party educational institutions. The Party decision calling for its establishment provided that the faculty should be recruited from the existing institutions of higher learning; it appears that a large number of the forty-three professors and *dotsents* teaching in 1948 had such a background. Many teach part-time in the Party School while retaining their regular chairs in Kiev University or in the Academy of Sciences of the Ukrainian S.S.R. In recent years there seems to have been an especially close relation between the Party School and the Kiev University Institute for Improving the Qualifications of Teachers of Marxism-Leninism. Those faculty members of the Higher Party School who did not have higher degrees apparently found it necessary to obtain them by studying in one of the established institutions. Two years after he became director, Chekaniuk took a candidate degree in the Institute of History of the Academy of Sciences, offering as his dissertation an expanded version of a propaganda pamphlet he had written during the war.[13]

Much of the basic curriculum in the Ukrainian Higher Party School resembles that in the Soviet universities. Among the required subjects are Logic, History of the U.S.S.R., History of International Relations, General History, Political Economy, Fundamentals of Soviet Economics, Political and Economic Geography, and Party Structure. In addition, Russian and Ukrainian language and literature are offered, as well as foreign languages, although not all students need take all of these courses.

This broad general training is of major importance for Party officials, for, as noted earlier, most officials must be sufficiently generalized in their abilities to cope with a wide range of situations. Such flexibility is no less important for the large number who had already attained a fairly high level of technical training before launching out on careers in the apparatus. Party discussions increasingly stress this theme:

> The second secretary of the L'vov gorkom of the Party, Comrade Mazur, who is in charge of questions of manufacturing, is an

engineer by training. However, he is not satisfied with this. During the past year he completed by correspondence the Higher Party School of the CPSU, attaining the candidate minimum. He reads a great deal of belletristic literature, investigates questions of economics and history. This enables him to give interesting reports, to present serious questions concerning the improvement of the work of manufacturing in the obkom bureau and in the Party press.[14]

While general education is important in the Higher Party School program, the Party does not neglect the special opportunity this period of training provides for heightening the official's indoctrination and for increasing his ability to act as an exponent of official ideology. Indicative of the importance of the ideological aspects of the Party training courses was the appointment of an important propaganda official, Ivan Alekseevich Sosnovskii, to teach Dialectical and Historical Materialism, which, along with the History of the VKP(b), was a required course for all students. Sosnovskii had been propaganda secretary of Zaporozh'e obkom and later became Deputy Director of the Propaganda and Agitation Section of the Central Committee. It is significant, nevertheless, that Sosnovskii did meet the requirements of academic training. Although he was of peasant origin (from the Urals) and had received all his schooling after joining the Party, he had gone far beyond the average apparatus official in his studies. While still in his twenties he had studied at what was then the principal center of Soviet Marxist study, the Institute of the Red Professors in Moscow; in 1947 he received the degree of candidate in philosophy.[15]

Important as are the broadening of the educational background and the strengthening of the ideological capacity of the official, the principal purpose of his stay at the Higher Party School is to make him more proficient in the performance of his duties in the apparatus. In a very real sense, therefore, this school and those at a lower level in which the students are given full-time, intensive training are professional training institutions. Because this aspect of the training program has a distinctly utilitarian purpose, each type of official follows a different curriculum. The school has two major divisions: the Party and the Soviet (state) faculties. The latter graduated 130 students in 1948, while the Party faculty graduated nearly 300. Students in the Soviet faculty had a specialized program, including such subjects as Constitutional Law and Soviet Structure, designed to increase their efficiency as general directors of state activities. Nearly half the students in the Party faculty, comprising Party and Komsomol "organizational" workers[16] (presumably secretaries and officials of the line and staff groups), pursued a fairly similar program.

Training for indoctrination specialists has, on the other hand, followed a considerably different pattern. Originally (1944) this division was set up as a distinct unit, the Republic School of Propagandists. At that time its student body of 331 propaganda specialists and 108 journalists was almost as large as the total of the Party School, but it was apparently of inferior quality. About 100 of the initial group "fell out" before completing the course, and many who were graduated did not enter Party work.[17] In the autumn of 1946 the Propagandists school was incorporated in the newly-formed Higher Party School. The enrollment was substantially reduced, the first graduating class of propagandists and journalists totaling only 165. The curriculum for indoctrination specialists continued, however, to be markedly different from that pursued by the generalists of the Party and state faculties.

The Party schools—and especially the Republic Higher Party School—have been regarded as the keystone of an in-service training program, rather than as institutions for preparing aspirants for careers in the apparatus. Alternation of intensive training with practical experience is a basic principle of the process of moulding the apparatus official. Normally, only those officials who have attained a fairly advanced post in the apparatus are accepted for the longer, full-time courses.

In 1947 the principal categories of students admitted to either the Higher Party School or the obkom school were those who were already serving as secretaries, directors of sections, instructors, or propagandists of the raikoms and gorkoms; Komsomol raikom and gorkom secretaries; raion newspaper editors; secretaries of large primary Party organizations; and chairmen, deputy chairmen, and department directors of raion executive committees. The obkoms acted as the initial selection agencies—each apparently being allotted a quota of students—though the Republic Party authorities reserved the power of confirmation.

TABLE 12

PARTY EDUCATION OF "DIRECTING CADRES"
IN THE UKRAINE*

(percentages)

Date	Higher Party Education	Incomplete Higher Party Education	Secondary Party Education
January 1, 1951	1.1	7.7	4.4
January 1, 1955	2.3	15.3	15.3

* Pinegin, p. 111. The source does not make clear the distinction between the various types of Party education; apparently "higher" education refers to the lengthier, fulltime courses discussed above.

As Table 12 shows, the proportion of Ukrainian officials who have completed a high level of Party training is still small, though it is growing rapidly. However, a significantly higher proportion of the major officials fall in this category. Thirty-nine and five-tenths per cent of the directors of obkom sections and 43 per cent of obkom secretaries had acquired Party training of this type by the beginning of 1955.[18] In early 1951 alone, two former first secretaries of obkoms and one former second secretary were enrolled in the regular course of the Republic Higher Party School, while two former first secretaries studied in the shorter courses. On completing their studies, most of these officials again filled important posts in the Party apparatus—one even returning to the first secretaryship of his former obkom. During the same general period, at least two other former obkom first secretaries were studying in the courses of the Central Committee of the VKP(b) in Moscow.

Withdrawal of such high-level officials from their responsibilities in order that they may take up to four years of training represents a heavy investment by the Party. Soviet analysts maintain, however, that the training system has proved itself by reducing the heavy turnover of officials which characterized the early postwar years.[19] At the same time they admit that at least in its early stages there was a high proportion of wastage among the students of the Party schools themselves; for example, 52 of the 146 graduates of the Zaporozh'e obkom course in 1946 returned to rank-and-file status in the Party.[20] At times the Party takes strong measures to impress its officials with the seriousness of the training program. In 1946 the "former" cadres secretary, the "former" deputy, and the chairman of the oblast executive committee were expelled from the Sumy obkom training courses for failure to progress in their studies.[21]

As noted earlier, a great many of the officials who have reached levels establishing their eligibility for attendance at the schools have come from working-class or peasant families. Such officials have little formal education except what they could attain after entering the apparatus. It is true that the Higher School required for admission completion of a secondary education, including specifically instruction in the Constitution of the U.S.S.R., geography, and the Russian and Ukrainian languages. In the years immediately following the war many officials of humble origins probably met these requirements in night classes, while the remaining prerequisite—completion of a course in the history of the CPSU—was doubtless met by Party indoctrination. At that time most of the courses were open to officials up to the age of forty. Since most officials in the immediate postwar period were young, there was time for many to complete these prerequisites.

While his case is probably not entirely typical, the background of Dmitri Gavrilovich Sadovnichenko indicates the training possibilities open to an official who had risen from the ranks. Born of a laboring-class family in Pavlograd, Sadovnichenko worked as a common laborer in his youth, then served as a sailor in the Black Sea Fleet. Until the war his Party career was limited, although he had finally become a raikom secretary just before the start of hostilities. Apparently he made his mark at the beginning of the German invasion when he worked behind the enemy lines as secretary of an underground obkom. While the war was still going on he was called to the Central Committee Secretariat, where he was employed for five years. Apparently the age limit of the Republic Higher Party School was rather flexible, for in 1948, when he was already forty-one, Sadovnichenko began training there. In 1950, after completing his course, he obtained the relatively important post of second secretary of Kamenets-Podolsk obkom.[22]

No doubt many rising officials make important contacts while students in the Republic Higher Party School or even catch the attention of their superiors by their performance as students. It seems doubtful, however, that men as old and as experienced in the apparatus as are the majority of the students develop a special *esprit de corps* or a feeling of distinctiveness from their period of study together. This generalization apparently holds for the state officials and for the portion of the Party trainees drawn from line and staff assignments who graduated from the Higher Party School before 1953. It is significant, however, that the officials preparing as propaganda or journalist specialists were considerably younger; at first, at least, an age limit of thirty-five was set for such applicants. Since the specialized courses for this group probably require a somewhat more advanced educational background, only those with some higher education are admitted. It seems likely that only those who were able to complete their formal preparation at a rather early age are likely to be able to enter upon the indoctrinational career. Moreover, indoctrination specialists appear to comprise a very high proportion of the officials who have obtained higher degrees in the ordinary educational institutions. Of the six officials of the Kharkov obkom apparatus with candidate degrees in 1955, four were in various aspects of indoctrinational supervision.[23] In general, it would appear that the more "professional" or specialized a group of officials becomes, the more it tends to become an elite by training.[24]

By 1956 the maximum age of thirty-five had been set as a requirement for all students entering the full-length courses of the Higher Party School and the inter-oblast schools.[25] It seems very likely that the proportion of students who have been favored enough to acquire a high degree of formal education in their youth has increased considerably. This tendency is likely to become more prominent as the emphasis on advanced general educational background and preparation for more specialized careers increases. There has been, moreover, a marked tendency to differentiate even rank-and-file Party members according to their educational attainments. As a secretary of the Party committee of Kiev city, Mariia M. Pidtychenko, put it:

. . . In the opinion of many propagandists the Party education of Communists ought to be organized in these stages. The first stage, for Communists who have elementary or incomplete secondary education, is to organize schools of political grammar with an obligatory test [*zachet*] or examination at the end of the instructional year. For this same portion of Communists it is essential to organize study of the biographies of V. I. Lenin and J. V. Stalin. The second stage, for Communists with secondary education, is to organize schools for study of the *Short Course in the History of the VKP(b)*, with obligatory examination at the end of the course. The third stage, for Communists with higher educations, consists of a profound study of dialectical and historical materialism and of the fundamentals of political economy at the level of the Evening University of Marxism-Leninism, with a two-year term of training.

For directing Party, Soviet, economic, and scientific workers and for directing workers in literature and in art, it is necessary to organize study of Marxist-Leninist theory at the level of the Higher Party School, with a three-year training term, including the passing of examinations and the obtaining of corresponding diplomas.

Of course, for the categories of Communists who have completed all stages of Party education it would be essential to organize study in special programs corresponding to the type of work and specialization of the Communist.[26]

More striking, however, was the proposal of this official that the Party Statutes (of the CPSU) be amended by a firm requirement that all Communists attain a secondary education:

In point "D" of Paragraph 3 of the Statutes it would consequently be added that a Communist must attain, as a minimum, a general secondary education.[27]

There is little doubt that the regime seems to be moving in the direction of an open recognition of the stratification of Soviet society according to educational attainments. Since most persons must receive their formal education while relatively young, the social position of most individuals will be determined before their careers are fairly started.

Any estimate of the effect of the increased educational attainments upon the official's loyalty to the Communist system is necessarily speculative. There are many elements in the training system which tend to prevent a development unfavorable to the regime. The high proportion of outright ideological indoctrination and the fact that all courses are taught from the Communist standpoint are powerful safeguards. Constant observation of the student is, of course, another safeguard. The fact that, up to the present at least, a large proportion of the student officials have come from obscure backgrounds and owe their entire cultural as well as political progress to the Party certainly tends strongly to induce their acceptance of its teachings.[28] Since the coming generation has frequently not had even second-hand contact with non-Communist cultural elements, one may expect that this tendency will in some ways grow even stronger. On the other hand, many observers have noted the tendency of the better-educated youth of the Soviet Union to become skeptical of its system. This skepticism seems to be especially prevalent among those who have had a considerable degree of exposure to the traditional subject matter of "liberal education" (history, literature, foreign languages), even though these subjects were taught from a Leninist viewpoint. The increasing emphasis on a rounded education for Party officials will tend to bring them into contact with these "dangerous" fields. The relation of an educated elite to a long-persisting, drastically totalitarian system remains a riddle which only the future can solve.

Footnotes to Chapter 3

1. M. S. Burmistenko, Speech to the Eighteenth Congress of the VKP(b), *Pravda*, March 17, 1939.
2. M. S. Burmistenko, "Partiinaia rabota—osnova nashikh pobed" [Party Work—The Basis of our Victories], *Partiinoe Stroitel'stvo*, No. 10, May, 1940, p. 8.
3. Speech of Khrushchev to the Sixteenth Congress, *PU*, January 27, 1949.
4. P. Iur, Secretary of L'vov obkom, "O krugozore rukovoditelia" [Concerning the Mental Outlook of the Director], *PU* January 27, 1956.
5. M. S. Burmistenko, "Smelee vydvigat' kadry" [Most Boldly Nominate Cadres], *Partiinoe Stroitel'stvo*, No. 5 March, 1939, p. 17.
6. *KPSU v resoliutsiiakh i resheniakh s"ezdov, konferentsii i plenumov TsK* [The CPSU in Resolutions and Decisions of the Congresses, Conferences, and Plenums of the Central Committee] (Moscow: Gosudarstvennoe Izdatel'stvo Politicheskoi Literatury, 1953), II, 1023.
7. *RU*, June 11, 1952.
8. See the notice on acceptance of students in *PU*, July 4, 1956.
9. *PU*, June 7, 1947.
10. See "Party Political Training in the Soviet Union," *Bulletin of the Institute for the Study of the History and Culture of the U.S.S.R.*, Vol. II, No. 8 (August, 1955), 29-33.
11. M. D. Men'shov, "Bor'ba kommunisticheskoi partii za sozdanie i vospitanie partiinykh i sovetskikh kadrov v zapadnykh oblastiakh Ukrainskoi SSR v chetvertoi piatiletke (1946-1950 gg.) [The Struggle of the Communist Party for Creating and Training Party and Soviet Cadres in the Western Oblasts of the Ukrainian S.S.R. in the Fourth Five-Year Plan (1946-1950)], an unpublished dissertation for obtaining the academic degree of candidate of historical sciences in the Institute for Improving the Qualifications of Teachers of Marxism-Leninism, Kiev State University, 1954, p. 129.
12. Unless otherwise indicated, the account of the Republic Higher Party School is based on newspaper accounts in *PU*, June 7, 1947; *RU*, July 29, 1948 and July 31, 1949; and *PU*, July 4, 1956; *KPSU v resoliutsiiakh*, II, 1023-25; M. D. Likhenko, "Bor'ba kommunisticheskoi partii Sovetskogo Soiuza za ideino-politicheskoe vospitanie rukovodiashchikh partiinykh i sovetskikh kadrov (1946-1950 gg.). Na materialiakh Ukrainy [The Struggle of the Communist Party of the Soviet Union for Idea-Political Education of Directing Party and Soviet Cadres (1946-1950). From Materials of the Ukraine], an unpublished dissertation for obtaining the academic degree of candidate of historical sciences in the Institute for Improving the Qualifications of Teachers of Marxism-Leninism, Kiev State University, 1935, pp. 79-80. It is also based on information given to me orally by Soviet educators in Kiev during the summer of 1956.
13. Mordukh Beniaminovich Pogrebinskii, "Trudiashchiesia Kieva i kievskoi oblasti v oborone stolitsy Ukrainskoi S.S.R." [The Toilers of Kiev and Kiev Oblast in the Defense of the Capital of the Ukrainian S.S.R.], an unpublished dissertation for obtaining the academic degree of candidate of historical sciences in the Academy of Sciences of the Ukrainian S.S.R., Kiev, 1953, p. xxiii.
14. P. Iur, *PU*, January 27, 1956.
15. See Sosnovskii's obituary in *PU*, February 20, 1953.

44 *The Soviet Bureaucratic Elite*

[16] Cf. Chapters 4 and 6.

[17] Likhenko, p. 89.

[18] *Ibid.*, p. 113.

[19] Likhenko. pp. 94-95.

[20] *Ibid.*, p. 89.

[21] *RU*, August 16, 1946. Similarly, the assistant procurator of Zaporozh'e city, the secretary of a city raikom, and other officials, were expelled from the Evening University there for non-attendance, See I. Lopach, "Vazhnoe zveno partiinogo prosveshcheniia" [An Important Link of Party Education], *PU*, May 30, 1953.

[22] See his obituary in *RU*, February 19, 1955.

[23] Pinegin, p. 114.

[24] Officers of the Red Army and of the Soviet foreign service have long been trained in special academies at a relatively early age.

[25] *PU*, July 4, 1956.

[26] Speech to Seventeenth Congress, *PU*, September 24, 1952.

[27] *Ibid.* Apparently Madame Pidtychenko meant point "E" of Paragraph 3, which read in both proposed and adopted versions: "[The member of the Party is obliged] to work to heighten his awareness, to master the fundamentals of Marxism-Leninism." See *KPSU v resoliutsiiakh*, II, 1123, and *Pravda*, October 14, 1952.

[28] See Fedorov's statement, quoted on pp. 48 ff.

4

Bosses of the Apparatus

THE HEART of the apparatus in the Ukraine is the generalist. Except at the lowest level, both the Party and state bureaucracies are organized on the territorial principle; each unit constitutes a province subject to the overall supervision of an individual official. These men—at the Republic and oblast levels a woman has never been given this responsibility—are responsible not for any specialized aspect of the system, but for its entire functioning. In American administrative terminology, they may appropriately be designated the "line officials."[1]

Because the Party bureaucracy is far more powerful than that of the state, the first secretary stands at the apex of the pyramid of line officials. Nikita Sergeevich Khrushchev, who occupied this post in the Ukrainian apparatus from 1938 until the end of 1949, would, therefore, have been the most important official considered in the present study even if he had not risen far higher after his departure from the Ukraine.

Khrushchev's importance to the elite of the Ukrainian apparatus has not arisen merely from his formal position in the Party. In many ways he has been at once the type and the model of the territorial boss. It is significant that almost his entire career has been spent in line posts. While Khrushchev began his Party career as a Red Army political worker during the Civil War, his first assignment in the apparatus (in 1925) was as secretary of a raikom, the basic unit in the territorial structure. He rose to successively higher positions in this structure: deputy chief (second secretary) of the Moscow gorkom in 1932; its first secretary in 1934; first secretary of the Moscow obkom in 1935; and first secretary of the KPU in January, 1938. Even after leaving the Ukraine, Khrushchev remained for a time director of a regional apparatus, for he was once again first secretary of the Moscow obkom as well as a subordinate secretary of the CPSU. Shortly after Stalin's death, he reached the apex of the Party pyramid as first secretary of the CPSU. In March, 1958, Khrushchev became chairman of the Council of Ministers of the U.S.S.R., thereby assuming—as he had for a time in the Ukraine after World War II—direct control of both the Party and the state bureaucracy.

Like many members of the elite, Khrushchev is a man of humble origins, having been born in a miner's family. What little formal training he has was obtained from the Party in a few years' study in the special schools set up for promising but uneducated Communists. While many line officials have a good deal more training and education than this, an official in a specialized branch of the apparatus could hardly attain prominence with so little. A line official, on the other hand, deals with the mass of the people; he manipulates the apparatus and, like political bosses elsewhere, his experience and common sense can be a sufficient basis for great success. In the Ukraine, even the supervision of the economy is comparatively easy for such a man, for the principal field of activity has been agriculture, the least technical aspect of economic life. It is significant that, since his departure from the Ukraine, Nikita Khrushchev, in addition to manipulating the Party machinery, has continued to be deeply concerned with agricultural problems.

Born in 1894, Khrushchev is a decade older than the typical member of the higher stratum of the elite. He is, however, no Old Bolshevik; he did not enter the Party until 1918, when the Revolution was an accomplished fact. Even after entering the Party, he remained in very obscure positions for a long time. In 1921, after demobilization from the Red Army where he had served as a political worker throughout the Civil War, he again worked for several years as a miner in the Donbas. His career in the apparatus did not begin until 1925, several years after Stalin had become General Secretary. Khrushchev took part in the struggle to establish Stalin as absolute dictator by fighting "right elements," and he was given his first major assignment in 1932 after Stalin's rivals had been beaten. Consequently, in spite of his age, Khrushchev fits the pattern of the elite which came to power after the Great Purge. His background is summed up neatly by the official biographical statement published when he arrived in the Ukraine in January, 1938:

> Comrade Khrushchev, who has gone through the school of combat and Party work, beginning at the very lowest, is an outstanding example of the post-October generation of Party workers trained by Stalin.[2]

Compared to Khrushchev, no other individual stands out in the Ukrainian apparatus, although there have been, of course, degrees of prominence. Two of his successors as first secretary, L. G. Mel'nikov and A. I. Kirichenko, enjoyed the additional prestige of belonging to the Presidium of the CPSU. As will appear later, however, the first secretaries of the KPU are only the most successful representatives of the group of obkom first secretaries.

A total of eighty-seven individuals served as obkom first secretaries between February, 1939, when relative stability was established in the oblast organization, and January, 1956. The posts held by sixty-one of these shortly before their appointment as first secretaries can be determined. Of these sixty-one, only twelve had been officials in the headquarters of the KPU, while the remainder occupied "field" posts in the oblasts.[3]

Most of those who worked in the oblasts had been in posts calling for the generalist's, rather than specialist's, skills; nearly half had acted either as heads of the oblast state bureaucracy or as deputies to an obkom first secretary. In about half the cases examined the immediate previous post of the first secretary had been in the same oblast. On the whole, therefore, the chief of the oblast is a man with broad experience, accustomed to directing the affairs of some considerable segment of the apparatus and frequently having experience in the immediate territory for which he is responsible as first secretary.

A considerable group of first secretaries have backgrounds closely resembling Khrushchev's. They are, of course, experienced in handling Party affairs, but they are not specialized in any aspect of its organization. While not much information is available on their earlier backgrounds, most would seem to be men of humble origin and little schooling. The most complete biographical sketch available, that of Aleksei Fedorovich Fedorov, probably contains a number of fairly typical features:

> I was a foundling. . . . I attended a two-year school. . . . When I was twelve I went to work as a herdsman's helper. At the beginning of 1920. . . I got the idea of volunteering for the Red Army. . . . I served until 1924, when I was demobilized. With that, my military career ended.
>
> I was twenty-three years old, but I had no trade, not even a particular goal. Yet one thing I knew, and knew for sure: I would make my way in life. I had a strong body and the Army had bred in me a strong will.
>
> I succeeded in getting a job as a timberer's helper on a tunnel construction job on the Merefa-Kherson railway. . . . It was here, on the tunnel job, that I acquired a real working-class schooling and a Bolshevik education. . . .
>
> Although I myself was eager to learn, the Soviet Government and the Party were even more eager to have people like me study and develop. . . . The Soviet person will find nothing particularly novel in my biography. It can be summed up in a few words: I was educated and led forward by the Party, by Soviet power. . . . I entered the third year of the Chernigov Building Trades Technical School. A year later I graduated, received my diploma, and had already begun to think further, to college, when my life took a different turn. I was called to the city Party committee and told:
>
> "People like you are needed for work in the rural districts."
>
> "What are 'people like me'?"
>
> "Of proletarian origin, reared on the job, devoted to the Party. . . ."
>
> Somewhat later I was elected second secretary of the district Party committee.
>
> The Party continued to keep an eye on me and helped me to develop. What theoretical background I lacked was supplied at courses arranged by the Central Committee in Kiev and subsequently at courses maintained in Moscow by the Central Committee of the [Communist Party of the Soviet Union (Bolshevik)].

> At the beginning of 1938 I was elected first secretary of the
> Chernigov Regional Committee [obkom] of the Communist
> Party (Bolsheviks) of the Ukraine.[4]

In view of Fedorov's "rough-and-ready" background, it is interesting to note that his first assignment was the direction of an
agricultural area. His subsequent post as obkom first secretary was
in an oblast which contains no major industries but is of considerable
agricultural importance. Fedorov set a record for the number of
oblasts in which he has held the position of first secretary; after
a period as partisan commander and head of the Volhynia underground obkom, he headed successively Kherson, Izmail, and
Zhitomir obkoms. All of these were areas in which agriculture
is by far the most important occupation.[5]

Fedorov was constantly preoccupied with agricultural matters:
"My mind was still full of the impressions of the trip: . . . the walls
of ripe wheat lining the road, the fields covered with low shrubs
of koksaghyz, the rubber-bearing plant we had just begun to cultivate
in the Chernigov region and of which we were so proud. . . ." But
he apparently had no training in agriculture and no farm experience other than his work as an adolescent agricultural laborer and
herdsman. This seems to be a typical pattern; Party leaders in agricultural regions are experienced directors, but they are not especially trained in agrarian problems.

A number of the obkom secretaries who, like Fedorov, have
"worked their way to the top" are transferred from one first secretaryship to another, nearly always in predominantly agricultural
oblasts. Some are permitted to direct the affairs of a single agricultural area for a long period. Two or three secretaries of agricultural oblasts have been promoted to become deputy chairmen
of the Council of Ministers or to one of the subordinate secretaryships of the Central Committee, where they have apparently
exercised a higher-level supervision over agriculture. While successful members of this group can anticipate long careers at the first-
secretary level, they rarely attain higher office.

Obkom first secretaries who are experienced in supervision of
industrial activities have a somewhat different career pattern.

Probably most of these men have considerably more education, including advanced technical training, than do secretaries in the "agricultural" group. Five of the obkom first secretaries have been definitely reported to be engineers by training, and of these all but one have directed major heavy industrial oblasts. In the U.S.S.R., training as an engineer by no means implies that a promising man will be limited to technical work or even primarily to the supervision of industrial activities. For a generation, such training has been regarded as the most desirable general preparation (other than specific training in the Party schools) for a young man hoping to reach a high position in any of the Soviet bureaucracies. In this respect, Soviet administrative practice contrasts sharply with that of many older bureaucracies, which have often tended to frown upon technical training for generalists who are to fill high supervisory posts.[6]

It is significant that Soviet writers who stress the increasing number of high Party line officials with higher education generally cite examples of those with engineering training. Apparently the only first secretary in the Ukrainian apparatus with a candidate degree (the highest degree awarded except to established scholars) is Vitalii Nikolaevich Titov, head of the Kharkov obkom apparatus, who obtained his degree in the Kharkov Engineering-Construction Institute.[7] Titov, who was a teacher before the war, is a rather unusual example of the technical theoretician who has attained high rank in the Party. The career of Leonid Il'ich Brezhnev, who next to Khrushchev and Kirichenko is the most prominent member of the Soviet elite to have risen through the Ukrainian apparatus, illustrates the more typical case of the practicing engineer who moves into Party direction. A graduate of the Dneprodzerzhinsk Metallurgical Institute, Brezhnev first attained a post of some significance in the apparatus in 1939 by making the rather unusual transition to the post of propaganda secretary in Dnepropetrovsk obkom. In the crisis of the war, however, he resumed engineering work as manager of a metallurgical plant in the Urals. Not long after the war Brezhnev became first secretary in Dnepropetrovsk oblast, industrially the second most important oblast in the Ukraine. In 1951 he left the Ukrainian apparatus to become first secretary of the Moldavian S.S.R. Shortly after Stalin's death he became chief of the political administration of the Red Fleet and soon afterwards second secretary of the Kazakh S.S.R. At the Twentieth Congress of the CPSU he was named a secretary of the Central Committee of the CPSU.

The value of a background in industrial direction is confirmed by the careers of two of the three obkom first secretaries who became first secretaries of the KPU. While nothing has been reported concerning Leonid Georgeevich Mel'nikov's education, the earliest apparatus post of importance which he held was that of director of the coal section of the Stalino obkom. Shortly afterwards (in 1939) he became a subordinate secretary of this obkom, which lies in the most important mining and manufacturing oblast of the Ukraine. From 1944 to 1947 he headed the obkom. In the latter year Mel'nikov became Khrushchev's deputy (second secretary of the KP[b]U); he took over direction of the Ukrainian Party when Khrushchev left for Moscow.

Mel'nikov was sharply attacked and dismissed from this post under rather obscure circumstances connected with Beria's bid for power and subsequent downfall in June, 1953. His successor, Aleskei Ilarionovich Kirichenko, was only thirty years old at the end of the Great Purge. Moreover, he had a rather late start in the apparatus, beginning his Party career as a member of the Party commission of a school for farm mechanics in 1936. Prior to that year Kirichenko had evidently been an obscure farm mechanic. Probably the first Ukrainian (by ethnic origin) to head the Ukrainian Party, Kirichenko claims a real proletarian background. The son of a railroad worker, he himself began work as a hired farm laborer at the age of eleven. Apparently he received no education after that time except in vocational and Party schools. Nevertheless, once in an apparatus job, Kirichenko rose rapidly; shortly before World War II he headed the Transportation Section of the Central Committee.[8] During the war he served as a member of the military councils at various fronts (in the same areas where Khrushchev was active). After a brief return to the Central Committee apparatus, Kirichenko became first secretary of the Odessa obkom. In 1949 he returned to the Central Committee as second secretary and succeeded Mel'nikov as first secretary in 1953; in December, 1957, he was promoted to Secretary of the Central Committee of the CPSU.

While Kirichenko has experience in several fields, his earlier background seems to place him in the group of line officials mainly concerned with Party direction and agriculture. The present first secretary, Nikolai Vitorovich Podgornyi, has been more deeply concerned, to judge from his speeches, with manufacturing and mining supervision. As permanent representative of the Council of Ministers of the Ukraine to the U.S.S.R. Council of Ministers, and later as first secretary of the industrial Kharkov and Dnepropetrovsk obkoms, he was also concerned with industrial managerial questions. Little has been revealed concerning his background, however.

An examination of the turnover in the first secretaryships illuminates several important facets of the elite of the Ukrainian apparatus. The average tenure of the obkom first secretary is slightly over three years, while the median tenure is between two and three years. Aside from the fairly remote danger to the regime of the creation of autonomous power centers, a "boss" as powerful as the first secretary might well come to treat the oblast as his personal property if he were allowed to direct its activities for a prolonged period. Consequently, though officials are probably often removed before they have become fully acquainted with a given territory, frequent transfer may, by discouraging laxity and favoritism, promote efficiency.

The three-year term of the obkom secretary seems to serve as a trial period for men who have just attained this level of the apparatus. Of the total number of individuals who occupied the position of obkom first secretary from January 1, 1939, to January 31, 1956, seventeen were still serving in their first assignment to this post on the latter date. Three of these had already served more than four years, however, and may be considered to have passed the probation period, as had, probably, the ten secretaries who previously served as first secretary in one or more other obkoms.

Twenty-four of the obkom first secretaries disappeared from public notice after serving a single assignment to this post. Of these, all but two had served less than four years. It seems likely that most of these men were considered failures in this important post and that they have not since been given major assignments. On the other hand, nine individuals were demoted to somewhat inferior but important posts, such as chairman of an oblast executive committee, after serving single assignments (often lengthy ones) as obkom first secretaries. Probably they were considered not fully capable of carrying the burden of overall responsibility for an oblast.

Seven first secretaries evidenced success in their first assignment by obtaining a transfer in grade to another obkom, but after several years in this second assignment they have not been mentioned. As several of these were criticized severely before disappearing, it seems that they, too, have been considered failures, though they passed the initial probation.

Twenty-one first secretaries have been promoted to more prominent positions in the Republic headquarters or outside the Ukraine, although some promotions seem to be primarily of an honorary nature. Of these twenty-one over a third had completed two or more assignments as obkom first secretaries before promotion, and most of the remainder had spent a considerable period of time in their single assignment as first secretary.

It appears that fourteen obkom secretaries, or about fifteen per cent of the group considered, are still on probation; thirty-four, or slightly less than half of the remainder, have been successful at least to the extent of maintaining their positions for a considerable period. The forty who have disappeared from public notice are generally those who apparently failed at a relatively short first assignment.

The period of probation of the obkom first secretary corresponds rather closely to the apparent rate of turnover in the upper levels of the elite as represented by the Central Committee. It would seem that the Party deliberately allows for about a fifty per cent "wastage" even among those considered reliable and capable enough to be assigned the great responsibility of supervising an entire oblast. Probably it is felt that only by giving an official such an extensive task can his mettle be fully tested. Those who meet the test, on the other hand, have a good chance of advancement or, at least, of indefinite tenure in similar posts.

Compared to those of the Party officials, the responsibilities of the state bureaucracy in the Ukraine are small. As will be discussed in the next chapter, its principal work has been direction of agriculture, as most of the more important industries were (until 1955) controlled by All-Union agencies centered in Moscow. In the fields directly affecting the average citizen, such as health, education, and housing, the Ukrainian state bureaucracy also exercises direct control—with apparently somewhat less Party supervision. The satisfaction of consumer wants, however, has for decades occupied a secondary position in the Soviet system.

At the apex of the Ukrainian state bureaucracy the Chairman of the Council of Ministers (until 1946 the Council of People's Commissars), Demian Sergeevich Korotchenko, held a position analogous to that held by Khrushchev in the Party. Korotchenko's occupancy of this post was not as continuous as was Khrushchev's of the first secretaryship, but it extended over a longer period. Born in the same year as Khrushchev, of a peasant family, Korotchenko also served in the Civil War and joined the Party in 1918. His career in the apparatus, however, began earlier, in 1919. From then on he frequently alternated between work in the Party line posts and positions in the state bureaucracy. In the middle thirties he worked under Khrushchev in the Moscow apparatus, but for a short time before going to the Ukraine in 1937 he had been first secretary of Smolensk obkom in the R.S.F.S.R. While Korotchenko's later career in the Ukraine centered around the chairmanship of the Council of Ministers (he held this post throughout most of 1938-1939 and from late 1947 until the end of 1953), it continued to exhibit the alternation between state and Party posts. From late 1939 until 1946, he was third secretary of the Party, and from 1946 until December, 1947, second secretary, or Secretary for Manufacturing.

The pattern of frequent transfer between Party and state positions is also found in careers of chairmen of the executive committees, the principal state officials at the oblast level. While the incomplete information available indicates that the previous posts most frequently held by the chairmen are the state offices of deputy chairman of the oblast executive committee and director of the oblast agricultural department, many have held subordinate obkom secretaryships or raikom first secretaryships.

In either an industrial or agricultural oblast the chairman has a fairly good chance to succeed to the post of first secretary; about one-eighth of the secretaries had just previously been chairmen of their own or another oblast. The average length of the chairman's assignment is about the same as that of the secretary: three years; and he is transferred to chairmanships in other oblasts fairly frequently. Unless he moves up through the first secretaryship, however, he seems to have a considerably smaller chance of a promotion to a top position in the Ukrainian apparatus.

While the police apparatus in the Ukraine is nominally subject to a member of the Republic Council of Ministers, it actually forms part of a separate and highly centralized All-Union apparatus. Consequently, police officials are frequently interchanged between the Ukraine and other parts of the Soviet Union. For this reason, and because very little information is published concerning these officials, it is impossible to discuss this group in detail.

The heads of the police apparatus in the Ukraine, the Ministers of Internal Affairs,[9] have, since the end of the Great Purge, apparently never been in a position of power approaching that of the Party leaders. The first, A. I. Uspenskii, evidently a protege of Ezhov, did not long outlast his sponsor. By 1940 Khrushchev was able to assert the primacy of the Party over the police in a sweeping fashion. Evidently the Commissar of Internal Affairs at that time, Ivan Aleksandrovich Serov, was amenable to playing a secondary role to the Party leaders. Serov has apparently continued his intimate working relationship with Khrushchev over the years. There is reason to suspect that Serov was associated with Khrushchev in the direction of the partisan movement during the war. Since the overthrow of Beria, Serov has apparently been regarded by Khrushchev and other Party leaders as the most reliable of professional policemen, for he has commanded Khrushchev's bodyguard on several of the latter's trips abroad and has been chosen to head the Committee on State Security of the U.S.S.R.

Nothing is known of Serov's early career, though his activities in Germany and the Baltic area suggest that he may have had experience in the military units of the police apparatus. Timofei Amvroseevich Strokach, who has been the Minister of the Interior of the Ukraine for almost the entire postwar period, is definitely one of the "military type" of police officers. Before 1939 he was an officer of the frontier guards, a special police formation organized on military lines to carry out the delicate task of sealing the borders of the U.S.S.R. During the war Strokach was chief of staff of the Ukrainian partisans.

Very little is known about MVD chiefs at the oblast level. Relatively, they probably occupy a somewhat stronger position than the Ukrainian Ministers of the Interior, for they are apparently always full members of the obkom bureaus, while the ministers have rarely been members of the Politburo or the Presidium. Except for two oblast MVD chiefs who were well-known partisan leaders, however, they have received practically no notice in the press.

There is, apparently, a special connection between the police apparatus and the Party organizations of the frontier oblasts. Definite evidence of this connection is available in the case of Mikhail Varnaevich Slon'. Slon' was one of the original group of apparatus officials appointed to the newly-created oblasts in territory acquired from Poland. After serving for a time as second secretary of Ternopol' obkom and later as chairman of the oblast executive committee, he became first secretary in Stanislav oblast, a highly strategic oblast because its rugged, forested terrain made it a principal center for Ukrainian nationalist partisan resistance to Soviet rule. Slon' was apparently not as successful in agricultural direction as in suppression of guerrilla activities. In 1948 he was temporarily relieved of his post after the Republic press had severely criticized the lag in collectivization of agriculture in the oblast. He regained his secretaryship a few months later, however, and continued in office until 1951, when he was transferred to the Republic MVD headquarters as deputy minister.[10]

The career of Mikhail Slon' is unusual in that the official held major line posts in three of the bureaucracies operating at the provincial level: police, state, and Party. As has been indicated, however, transfer between the state and Party service is very frequent for officials who rise to direct either of these bureaucracies at the oblast or Republic level. These line officers appear to be fitted by training and experience primarily for the overall direction of the apparatus, especially its supervision of the economy. Direction of more specific phases of Party activities is usually left to men with more specialized training. The line "generalists," however, appear to have much the better chance of attaining the most important positions in the apparatus. They are, to be sure, on probation even after they have attained the highest posts in the oblast bureaucracies, and many of those who successfully pass never rise above this level. Most of the top positions in the Ukrainian apparatus—and a considerable number in the U.S.S.R. as a whole—are, however, filled from their ranks.

Footnotes to Chapter 4

1. On the line officials, see especially Merle Fainsod, *How Russia is Ruled* (Cambridge, Mass.: Harvard University Press, 1954), pp. 189-196; and Sidney Harcave, *Structure and Functioning of the Lower Party Organizations in the Soviet Union* (Maxwell Air Force Base, Alabama: Human Resources Research Institute; Technical Research Report Number 23, January, 1954), pp. 15-16.

2. *Visti*, January 28, 1938. Most of the details on Khrushchev's early career are taken from this statement.

3. Including two who held posts in oblasts of the R.S.F.S.R.

4. A. Fedorov, *The Underground Committee Carries On* (Moscow: Foreign Languages Publishing House, 1952), pp. 33-38.

5. The construction of a large-scale hydroelectric project which may change the Kherson oblast economy began after Fedorov's tour of duty there.

6. "If the administrative staff [of the Post Office] were recruited in part from technicians, a body of quasi-experts would grow up in the Secretariat who would tend to press their views on technical matters, possibly in opposition to those of the technical department." See *Minutes of Evidence* (1930) of the Royal Commission on the Civil Service, quoted in R. K. Kelsau, *Higher Civil Servants in Britain: From 1870 to the Present Day* (London: Routledge and Kegan Paul Ltd., 1955), p. 114.

7. I. T. Pinegin, "Rabota KP Ukrainy po osushchestvleniiu reshenii partii o podbore, rasstanovke i vospitanii rukovodiashchikh partiinykh i sovetskikh kadrov v poslevoennyi period (1946-1955 gg.)" [The Work of the Communist Party of the Ukraine in Carrying Out the Decisions of the Party Concerning the Selection, Assignment, and Training of Directing Party and Soviet Cadres in the Postwar Period (1946-1955)], an unpublished dissertation for obtaining the academic degree of candidate of historical sciences in the Academy of Social Sciences of the Central Committee of the CPSU, Moscow, 1955, p. 99.

8. *Komunist*, March 12, 1941; *Pravda*, December 22, 1957 (from which most of the biographical information given above is drawn) does not mention this post but speaks of Kirichenko as a "sector director," "department director," and "secretary" (after February, 1941) of the Central Committee. Transportation, because of its strategic importance, has always occupied a special place in the Party system and is closely related to the police. It is interesting to note that another former director of the Transportation Section, Vitalii Fedotovich Nikitichenko, recently became chairman of the Committee on State Security, one of the principal police agencies.

9. Known before 1946, of course, as People's Commissars. Between February and July, 1941, and again from April, 1943, to March, 1953, this Ministry was subdivided into the Ministry of Internal Affairs and the Ministry of State Security (MGB); since April, 1954, there has been a Committee on State Security carrying on some of the functions of the former MGB. While the MGB was probably a more important organization than the MVD, very little information is available concerning its Ukrainian branch. On the general position of the police apparatus, see especially Fainsod, pp. 354-389; Boris Meissner, *Russland im Umbruch* (Frankfurt a/M: Verlag für Geschichte und Politik, 1951), pp. 30-32; Zbigniew K. Brzezinski, *The Permanent Purge* (Cambridge, Mass.: Harvard University Press, 1956), pp. 158-163; and Simon Wolin

and Robert M. Slusser, editors, *The Soviet Secret Police* (New York: Frederick A. Praeger, 1957).

10. This information is based primarily on the obituary of Slon' in *RU*, April 21, 1955. This statement does not mention his prewar posts or his replacement after criticism in 1948.

5

Supervising the Economy

NEXT to the maintenance of political control, the operation of the economy is the chief concern of the Soviet regime. Indeed, the press and even Party meetings devote more attention to economic matters than to the political and ideological questions. As was pointed out in the preceding chapter, a major part of the responsibility of the Party first secretaries at each level of the apparatus is the supervision of production.

Nevertheless, there is considerable ambiguity in the relationship of the Party to economic activities. A Party line official is responsible for the successful operation of economic enterprises in his area, but he has no formally defined authority over most of them. His nominal role is to aid, to stimulate, to observe, and to check economic enterprises, but not to take over their management.

> The Party director is not an administrator. His mutual relations with the people are not based upon the force of an order, but [upon] the authority and force of the Party organization standing behind him, [and upon] his nearness to the laborers, the collective farm workers, and the employees. The able worker acts as a militant organizer of the masses, as their political educator.[1]

In fact, the great power in the hands of the territorial boss, and his own keen awareness that his future depends on the success of his area's economy, frequently lead him to overstep these bounds. Consequently, complete analysis of power relationships in this field would have to be based on exhaustive empirical examination of the functioning of the apparatus. Such a study obviously lies beyond the scope of this work. Nevertheless, a realistic appraisal of the Ukrainian apparatus elite requires at least a summary examination of the interaction between economic management and the elite power structure.[2]

The role of the Ukrainian apparatus in the economy stands forth most clearly in the direction of agriculture. In the Soviet rural scene, especially in the Ukraine, political and economic aspects are almost inextricably mingled; indeed, the economic is often the obverse side of the political. While the share of the Ukraine in the total agricultural production has gradually declined, it still constitutes a crucial element. In 1955 the Ukraine contained one-sixth of the total area of the U.S.S.R. devoted to crops, including one-seventh of the wheat fields.[3] The yield of these areas, much more fertile and favored by a better climate than the average, was relatively still higher, comprising one-fifth of the agricultural production of the U.S.S.R. in recent years.[4]

The inability to achieve substantial increases in agricultural production is probably the greatest single weakness of the Soviet system. This failure is in large part a reflection of a political failure— the inability to enlist the enthusiasm, or, at least, the active co-operation of the peasantry. The fact that it was essentially an urban movement, dominating a hostile, or at best a passive, countryside, hampered the Communist Party from the beginning of its rule in the Ukraine. During the Civil War and the collectivization campaign, the Party had to utilize forces from the cities (largely non-Ukrainian in nationality) and from outside the Ukraine to carry out its programs. Even in the years immediately following the Great Purge, the Party could not have members in each collective farm (kolkhoz), the principal unit of agricultural production. The centers of Party organization were in the sovkhozes (state farms), Machine Tractor Stations (MTS), and the communes (territorial subdivisions of the raion).[5] In the postwar years the situation of the Party improved considerably, principally through the dispatch of thousands of urban members to the rural districts. In 1948 alone, Poltava and Kharkov oblasts each increased kolkhoz Party organization membership by over 1,000.[6] By 1948 the 700-odd rural raions contained 327,100 Communists, almost half of the entire Ukrainian Party, though only forty per cent were actually employed in agricultural enterprises.[7] By 1949

about sixty per cent of the kolkhozes contained Party organizations, and the same proportion had Party members as chairmen.[8]
This seemed, however, to represent the maximum diversion of
personnel to the rural areas which the Party could afford. If the
goal of direct Party supervision over each unit of agricultural production and each community of peasants were to be attained, the
number of units had to be reduced. Such reasoning appears to
have motivated the drastic consolidation of kolkhozes in 1950,
which reduced the number to 7,182, about one-fourth of the 1949
total.[9] The continued dependence of the Party in the rural areas
upon its urban base is indicated, however, by the dispatch in 1955
of "the thirty thousand" Communists and Komsomols to the
rural areas in a renewed effort to raise farm production.

The weak position of the Party at lower levels of the rural structure has endowed the first secretary of the rural raikom with a
peculiar importance in the economic field. While his powers over
agricultural work are nominally no greater than those of higher
Party officials over economic activities in their areas, in practice
the raikom secretary appears to manage, as well as to supervise,
farm production. To some extent this responsibility is shared with
the raion executive committee chairman; the specialists in agricultural work—the director of the raion agricultural department
and the director of the raikom agricultural section—hold distinctly
inferior positions. They rarely receive prominent notice or promotion. On the other hand, while the vast majority of raikom
secretaries do not rise in the Party pyramid, those who achieve
outstanding success in agricultural direction apparently have an
excellent chance to attain a position in the middle level of the
elite.[10]

The same general pattern prevails at the obkom level. In the
predominantly agricultural oblasts the principal figures in supervision of farm activities are the first secretary and the chairman
of the executive committee. The director of the oblast agricultural
department is frequently an official of some importance. He may
be a member of the oblast executive committee, though not of
the obkom bureau. The director of the obkom agricultural section
is usually a person of minor importance; however, one of the sub-

ordinate obkom secretaries is frequently primarily concerned with agricultural supervision.

In contrast to the situation at the oblast and the raion levels, the Republic headquarters contains a group of powerful officials whose sole responsibility is the direction of agriculture. The Agricultural Section of the Central Committee Secretariat has always been headed by an official of third-rate importance in the elite, though occasionally this post has been the stepping-stone to a major position in the apparatus. The state officials in agricultural direction, on the other hand, have been men of very considerable importance; as a group, they are probably second in importance only to the obkom first secretaries. The principal post at the Republic level is the Ministry of Agriculture, a Republic agency. The Ministry of Sovkhozes, a Union-Republic Ministry (i.e., one formally subordinate to a corresponding ministry in Moscow, as well as to the Council of Ministers of the Ukrainian Republic) is also very important. A third agency of key significance until 1955 was the Ministry of Procurements, charged with collection of state quotas of produce. An All-Union Ministry, it was represented in the Ukraine by a "plenipotentiary" to the Council of Ministers and by similar officials at lower levels of the territorial apparatus. In addition, there have been from time to time ministries for special branches of agricultural production or processing, such as the Ministry for Meat and Milk Production.

In spite of the complexity of its relationship to the Ukrainian Council of Ministers, this group of agencies appears to operate to a considerable degree as a unit. There has been a high degree of interchange of top personnel among these agencies, including even the post of plenipotentiary of the Ministry of Procurements. For example, Vasili Dmitreevich Kalashnikov, who had been plenipotentiary for many years, became Deputy Minister of Agriculture and Procurements in 1953 when the Republic Ministry of Agriculture was temporarily given this new designation. In 1954, with the old nomenclature restored, Grigori Prokof'evich Butenko, who had earlier been Minister of Agriculture and Minister of Meat and Milk, became plenipotentiary.[11]

The average tenure of these top officials (including ministers and deputy ministers) in a given position is three to four years, i. e., about the same as that of the obkom first secretary or the oblast executive committee chairman. Since, however, the Republic-level agricultural officials tend to be transferred among the agencies in this field, they are likely to spend a considerably longer period in the high-level direction of farm activities.

The Republic agricultural officials are immediately responsible for agricultural activities—other than for the operation of the kolkhozes, which are nominally cooperative associations. The state officials direct the network of collection points, the MTS, and the agronomists who instruct the peasants in proper farm techniques and, in addition, directly operate the state farms. One of the puzzles of the Soviet system is the delimitation of authority between these officials and the oblast and raion authorities discussed earlier. Apparently there is no precise boundary; a shifting adjustment is influenced by personalities, practical exigencies, and power constellations. One clue to the nature of the relationship is provided, however, by the fact that there is a very frequent interchange of personnel between the two groups. The present Minister of Agriculture, Mark Sidorovich Spivak, for example, once served as an obkom secretary in Stalino, and later in Poltava. At least three of those who have been deputy ministers in the agricultural agencies had earlier been obkom first secretaries, while one subsequently became a first secretary. The interchange of personnel between the field posts most important in agricultural direction and the Republic offices has probably led to a mutual increase in understanding; it has also, no doubt, influenced officials to avoid clashes with those with whom they may expect to serve at a subsequent stage of their careers.

If it is difficult to delimit areas of authority in agricultural direction, it is far harder to do so in industry. While overall policy for agriculture, as for other aspects of Soviet life, is made in Moscow, the agencies in immediate control are at least part of the Ukrainian apparatus. Until 1955, on the other hand, the agencies in immediate control of the most important branches of industry were in Moscow. All heavy industry was divided among a number of All-Union ministries, which, of course, carried on operations throughout the U.S.S.R. but were not subject to the Councils of Ministers in the Union Republics. While the Union-Republic Ministry (with a ministry in the Republic capital as well as a corresponding one in Moscow) directed light industry, Moscow controlled most of the enterprises in the field until 1956.

The Ukrainian apparatus, and the Party in particular, has not been entirely detached even from heavy industry. The primary Party organizations, which exist in every important plant, are subject to the territorial Party organizations. Consequently, the working forces of the factories are brought in contact with the Ukrainian Party even though formally it has no right to interfere in management. The secretaries of most of the plant organizations are paid Party functionaries, i. e., officials of the apparatus. While they do not have any right to interfere in factory management, they may keep higher Party authorities informed on this subject; at times the plant manager may feel it wise to accept their advice. As will appear later, however, the manager of a major heavy industrial enterprise in the Ukraine appears to enjoy much more prestige even in Party circles than does the secretary of the Party organization in his plant. Moreover, the most important enterprises are assigned a more important official: "the organizer of the Central Committee of the CPSU," who, in effect, bypasses the Ukrainian apparatus altogether.[12]

The more important plant managers seem to have more influence than even the lower level of territorial secretaries with whom they come in contact. A factory usually is located in a large city. The unit of Party territorial organization there is the urban raikom, in an area analogous to the ward of an American city. In cities like Kiev and L'vov, most industrial enterprises and other establishments have few workers. Consequently, many of the primary Party organizations are small and the raikom first secretary has an important coordinating function. Frequently he is promoted to an office of considerable significance in the apparatus; at least five Kiev raikom secretaries became secretaries of the gorkom. In cities where industrial operations are on a larger scale, the raikom secretary tends to be overshadowed by the plant managers and, perhaps, by the plant Party secretaries; he seems rarely to move to higher posts. If the raikom secretary endeavors to intervene in industrial operations, he risks a severe rebuke. For example, the secretary of Krasnogvardeisk raikom in Dnepropetrovsk was sharply criticized for intruding upon the province of an All-Union Commissariat by urging the Party organization in a factory to consider removal of the manager.[13]

TABLE 13

ECONOMIC ENTERPRISE MANAGERS ELECTED TO
THE CENTRAL COMMITTEE OF THE K.P.U.*

	1938	1940	1949	1952	1954	1956
Coal combine or trust directors	–	4	4	2	2	–
Rail district directors	1	1	2	1	2	2
Metal factory directors	–	1	2	3	2	1
Machinery factory directors	–	–	1	2	3	3
Hydroelectric construction project directors	–	–	–	3	3	2
Sugar combine directors	1	1	–	–	–	–
Total	2	7	9	11	12	8

* The figures include both members and candidates of the Central Committee. It is very likely that most of the figures cited are considerably lower than the actual number of enterprise managers in each category, for, as noted earlier (Chapter 2, n. 8), a large number of members and candidates cannot be identified. Since, however, those who could be identified are those who received some publicity during the period before or after the election of the Central Committee in which they were listed, the figures at least serve as a rough guide to the relative prominence of managers in the various categories shown. Included among "Coal combine or trust directors" is one chief engineer of a trust.

In contrast to the Party officials with whom they are in direct contact, the managers of the great heavy manufacturing enterprises, jokingly referred to as the "kings,"[14] are more prominent than any other officials except those at the top obkom and Republic levels. As Table 13 indicates, managers have increasingly attained places in the Central Committee, a recognition of their importance even in purely Party affairs. In contrast, only one secretary of a factory Party organization has ever attained such rank at the KPU Congresses. Moreover, the manager, especially if he is an old and trusted Party member, may share with the secretary the organization and the conduct of indoctrination activities within the factory.[15]

For all the recognition accorded them in Party circles, industrial managers do not seem to play a major part in deciding the most important questions taken up by the Central Committee. The absence of managers from discussions in the Central Committee is partly a result of the fact that this body does not discuss in detail the plans and management of heavy industry, which, of course, lie outside its competence. Nevertheless, one might anticipate that managers would play an important part in resolving matters of considerable indirect interest to their plant operations, such as organization of retail trade, increase of consumers' goods, and the development of municipal economics and housing. In fact, however, the managers on the Central Committee have not participated in discussion of these topics.[16]

The industrial managers, moreover, have been conspicuously absent in the Central Committee's considerations of indoctrinational questions. Even on a subject of such direct interest to plant management as "Cultural-Educational Work Among Factory Workers in Voroshilovgrad and Mariupol' [Zhdanov]," the gorkom first secretaries presented the reports while the managers were absent.[17] The higher Party officials appear to maintain control over all matters outside the sphere of enterprise management itself.

While the generally dominant position of the Ukrainian apparatus vis-à-vis plant managers is clearly evident in all spheres save industrial operation itself, Party, state, and industrial directors in the Donbas appear to have been in a somewhat peculiar position. This area, the most important coal mining and industrial center of the Ukraine, forms an economic unit with Rostov oblast of the R.S.F.S.R. In both the direction of coal mining and in Party organization, officials have been interchanged frequently between Rostov and the Ukrainian Donbas oblasts (Stalino and Voroshilovgrad). There is some evidence, though it is far from conclusive, that both economic management and Party leadership in this area were linked to the Soviet power alignment headed by Georgi Malenkov.

In addition to the ordinary channels of Party activity, the higher levels of the Ukrainian Party have certain special agencies to aid in the task of supervising and stimulating industry. Until 1939 the Central Committee Secretariat, the obkoms, and the gorkoms contained a number of sections devoted to particular branches of industry. In 1939, in accordance with the shift to "functionalism" in Party organization, these sections were generally abolished.[18] Some remained at the obkom level, however, and the "industrial-branch" sections, as they were called, were generally restored at the end of 1948. The position of the officials in charge of these agencies appears always to have been an uneasy one. They cannot intervene in the management of the plant, yet they share some responsibility for its success. The approach of some section directors was to turn themselves into expediters or trouble-shooters among plants in their branches of industry. This practice was, however, sharply criticized as exceeding the authority of the director[19].

In most instances, the heads of these sections, either at the obkom or Central Committee level, have been minor figures who have not risen in the apparatus. The directors of the sections for transportation and coal production have, however, been notable exceptions to this generalization. It should also be noted that there have been certain high officials in the Council of Ministers—particularly D. S. Korotchenko when he was chairman, and certain deputy chairmen such as I. S. Senin—who have been especially qualified to supervise industrial activities in general and have exerted themselves in this field.

Beginning in 1955, far-reaching changes were made in the formal organization of the Soviet industrial system. Two of the most important All-Union ministries for heavy industry—Coal and Heavy Metallurgy—were transformed into Union Republic ministries. In June, 1956, many industrial enterprises which had been controlled by ministries in Moscow were transferred to the corresponding ministries in the Union Republics. A year later many of the Union Republic ministries themselves were abolished, and primary direction of industry was delegated to Councils of Popular Economy (sovnarkhozes) in each of eleven districts into which the Ukrainian S.S.R. was divided.

These changes were closely connected to the power struggle between Khrushchev and his rivals. The nominal decentralization of control over industry was probably designed to decrease the power of the Moscow industrial management corps, which apparently tended to support Malenkov and Lazar Kaganovich, while increasing the authority of Khrushchev's strong adherents among the territorial Party bosses. That the latter profited by the formation of the sovnarkhozes is suggested by several appointments, such as that of I. I. Diadik, a secretary of the Stalino obkom, to the post of chairman of the Stalino sovnarkhoz. In general, however, the reshuffling of economic control agencies does not appear to have been of major political significance in the Ukraine, where, by 1956, Khrushchev's followers already seem to have been strongly entrenched throughout the economic system. For example, four deputy chairmen of the Ukrainian Council of Ministers, made redundant by the changes, were almost immediately appointed deputy chairmen of the Gosplan (State Planning Committee) which assumed many of the economic control functions in Kiev.[20]

Footnotes to Chapter 5

1. L. Slepov, *Mestnye partiinye organy: Lektsii prochitannye v Vyshei Partiinoi Shkole pri TsK KPSS, Kafedra Partiinogo Stroitel'stva* [Local Party-organs: Lectures Delivered in the Higher Party School of the Central Committee of the CPSU, Department of Party Structure] (Moscow: Vyshaia Partiinaia Shkola pri TsK KPSS, 1954), p. 41.

2. On the interaction of Party, state, and economic agencies, see especially Merle Fainsod, *How Russia is Ruled* (Cambridge, Mass.: Harvard University Press, 1954), Chapters XV and XVI; Sidney Harcave, *Structure and Functioning of the Lower Party Organizations in the Soviet Union* (Maxwell Air Force Base, Alabama: Human Resources Research Institute; Technical Research Report Number 23, January, 1954), pp. 40-43; Alexander Vucinich, *Soviet Economic Institutions* (Stanford, California: Stanford University Press, 1952); Harry Schwartz, *Russia's Soviet Economy*, 2nd ed. (New York: Prentice-Hall, 1954), Chapters 6 and 8; Alexander Baykov, *The Development of the Soviet Economic System* (New York: The Macmillan Co., 1947), Chapter 16; David Granick, *Management of the Industrial Firm in the U.S.S.R.: A Study in Soviet Economic Planning* (New York: Columbia University Press, 1954), especially Chapter 12; and Gregory Bienstock, Solomon M. Schwarz, and Aaron Yugow, *Management in Russian Industry and Agriculture* (New York: Oxford University Press, 1944).

3. Tsentralnoe Statisticheskoe Upravlenie pri Sovete Ministrov S.S.S.R., *Narodnoe khoziastvo S.S.R.: statisticheskii sbornik* [The National Economy of the U.S.S.R.: A Statistical Yearbook] (Moscow: Gosudarstvennoe Statisticheskoe Izdatel'stvo, 1956), pp. 112-113.

4. N. I. Lialikov, *Sovetskaia Ukraina: Ocherk ekonomicheskoi geografii* [The Soviet Ukraine: A Sketch of Economic Geography] (Moscow: Gosudarstvennoe Izdatel'stvo Geograficheskoi Literatury, 1954), p. 6.

5. See the speech of S. B. Zadionchenko, first secretary of the Dnepropetrovsk obkom, to the Eighteenth Congress of the VKP(b), *Pravda*, March 13, 1939.

6. Speech of V. M. Churaev to the Sixteenth Congress, *PU*, January 28, 1949; Report of Poltava oblast Party Conference, *PU*, January 13, 1949.

7. "O vosstanovlenii i pod"eme sel'skogo khoiaistva i partiino-politecheskoi rabote na sele" [On the Restoration and Rise of Agriculture and Party-Political Work in the Village], *Partiinaia Zhizn'*, No. 5, March, 1948, p. 11.

8. Based on comparison of a large number of isolated data.

9. K. Isaeva, *Tsvetushchaia Ukraina: ocherk o dokumental'nom fil'me* [The Flowering Ukraine: A Sketch of a Documentary Film] (Moscow: Goskinoizdat, 1952), p. 20.

10. It has been impossible to trace the careers of the thousands of raikom first secretaries in the Ukraine between 1938 and 1956. Several comparisons of lists of secretaries and lists of officials in "middle-level" elite posts indicate that a fairly large proportion of the latter are drawn from raikom secretaries, though, in view of their numbers, the vast majority of the latter cannot secure such promotions. For example, of several hundred raikom secretaries awarded decorations for reconstruction of agriculture at the end of the war, only seven have been found to attain middle-level positions in the Ukrainian apparatus up to 1957. They include, however, several prominent members of the present elite such as Central Committee Secretary N. D. Bubnovskii, and I. I. Sta-

fiichuk, chairman of the Kiev oblast executive committee. Promotion within the raikom apparatus is considerably more frequent; in 1938, 149 raikom second secretaries (about 25 per cent) became first secretaries, while 98 third secretaries (about 17 per cent) became second or first secretaries. See M. S. Burmistenko, "Smelee vydvigat' kadry" [Most Boldly Nominate Cadres], *Partiinoe Stroitel'stvo*, No. 5 (March, 1939), p. 15.

11. In 1956 Butenko returned to the Republic state bureaucracy as Minister of Grain Products and later became Deputy Chairman of the Council of Ministers.

12. Sometimes, however, these organizers are former officials of the Ukrainian apparatus.

13. "Mestnaia partiinaia khronika" [Local Party Chronicle]. *Partiinoe Stroitel'stvo*, No. 18 (September, 1940), pp. 62-63.

14. Natan Rybak, *Oruzhie s nami* [Arms With Us] (Moscow: Izdatel'stvo TsK VLKSM "Molodaia Gvardiia," 1944), p. 10.

15. See A. Iashchenko, "Vospitanie novykh kadrov rabochevo klassa" [Education of the New Cadres of the Working Class], *PU*, August 21, 1952; *PU*, July 18, 1945.

16. *PU*, December 27, 1952; July 1, 1953; June 9, 1945.

17. *RU*, May 19, 1946. Voroshilovgrad was renamed Lugansk in 1957.

18. See Chapter 6.

19. M. Sharaban, "Viddil obkomu chy arbitrazhna komisiia" [A Section of the Obkom or an Arbitration Commission], *Komunist*, July 15, 1940.

20. *RU*, July 18, 1957.

6

Mechanisms of Control

$\mathbf{A}$LONGSIDE the main channel of Party authority comprising the first secretaries are a number of auxiliary Party branches. Among the most important are those which would be called in American administrative terminology the "staff" agencies. The basic purpose of the staff agencies is to see that the Party machinery functions efficiently in response to the will of the central authorities. These branches of the apparatus do not themselves supervise the activities of the population in general, or the economy, but they endeavor to ensure that the Party and the other control organizations are in a position to do so.[1]

During the period between 1938 and 1941 the staff agencies occupied an unusually important role in the Ukrainian apparatus, for the wholesale depletion of the upper and middle levels of the Party and state hierarchies by the Great Purge necessitated sweeping replacement of personnel and close supervision and instruction of the newly-appointed officials. During and immediately after the Purge, the tasks of personnel assignment and organizational supervision within the Party ("internal" Party affairs) were assigned to the Section of Directing Party Organs, while corresponding tasks for state and economic institutions were allocated to the "industrial" sections of the Party Committees. In March, 1939, these functions were divided between a cadres (personnel) section and an organization-instruction section; the jurisdiction of the new sections extended to the state and economic bureaucracies as well as to the Party itself, however.[2]

In spite of the division of the staff functions, overall direction of these tasks continued to be in the hands of a single official, the second secretary of the KP(b)U, Mikhail Alekseevich Burmistenko.

Burmistenko was one of the most enigmatic figures of the Ukrainian Party, if not of the entire Soviet regime. While he arrived in the Ukraine at the same time as Nikita Khrushchev (January, 1938), Burmistenko's earlier background was quite dissimilar. From 1936 until 1938 he had been a subordinate official of the Section of Directing Party Organs of the VKP(b), then directed by Georgi M. Malenkov, who was rapidly rising as a protege of Stalin. Earlier, Burmistenko had had experience in almost all aspects of political work in the lower echelons; he had held posts successively in the territorial Party apparatus, the Red Army political administration, and in Party journalism. In view of the close association of the Section of Directing Party Organs with the NKVD in the Purge process, however, it may be significant that he had started his Party career in 1919 at the age of seventeen by joining the Cheka.

In spite of his typically Ukrainian name, Burmistenko was born near Saratov on the Volga. The fact that he was for a time an editor in the German Autonomous Republic in that region suggests that he may have been partly of German ancestry, or at least that he had early German associations. His only major assignment outside Moscow before his dispatch to the Ukraine was as secretary of the Kalmyk A.S.S.R., another area troublesome to the central authorities because of its nationalist tendencies. Probably Burmistenko's lack of previous association with the Ukraine (and his long career at the center) made him appear a particularly desirable choice for a role in the delicate task of rebuilding the Ukrainian apparatus in conformity to the wishes of Stalin and his associates. Quite possibly Stalin also regarded him as a useful counterweight to Khrushchev, with his long career in the territorial apparatus.

While Burmistenko's chief interest was personnel, his speeches and articles reveal a general concern with the organization and functioning of the Party machine. This was true both during the period when these aspects were combined and after the formation of the cadres and organization-instruction sections. At the Fifteenth Ukrainian Party Congress, as well as in a number of special meetings and in articles published over his signature in

the Party press, Burmistenko analyzed all phases of these subjects and interpreted the policy to be pursued by the Ukrainian
Party in carrying out the decisions of Moscow.

   Although he was always exceeded in prominence by Khrushchev, Burmistenko dominated the field of internal Party operations
down to the outbreak of the war. When hostilities began he was
active in organizing the underground and partisan movements,
and apparently remained in Kiev or the vicinity until the area
was almost surrounded by the German forces.[3] Then he disappeared. From time to time Soviet works have mentioned him in a
laudatory though brief manner but his name has neither reappeared
among the lists of Soviet officials nor has any account of his fate
been published.

   While Burmistenko dominated the staff agencies until his disappearance, the cadres secretary of the Central Committee, Moisei
Semenovich Spivak, was an important member of the top echelon
of the Ukrainian Party. During the Purge period, Spivak, a Jew,
had risen rapidly from an obscure post in the Kiev city Party
apparatus. Described by an acquaintance as a "civilian-type
Chekist," he also apparently participated in the close collabora-
tion with NKVD officials which seems to have characterized many
cadres officials during the war and prewar periods.[4] During the war
Spivak continued to direct cadre selection, probably in connection
with the partisan movement. After the war, however, he was transferred to a line position, as first secretary of Zhitomir obkom.[5]

   Compared to the cadres secretary, the director of the organization-instruction section of the Central Committee Secretariat,
Andrei Nikoforovich Zlenko, was a relatively minor personage.
Only a candidate of the Central Committee in 1940, Zlenko served
as director until 1947, when he was transferred to another staff
position as inspector of the Central Committee.[6] In 1951 he continued to direct staff agencies as second secretary of L'vov obkom,
and more recently he has taken still another position of an organizational nature as Secretary of the Presidium of the Supreme Soviet.

   Burmistenko's disappearance substantially altered the position
of the staff agencies. Apparently Nikita Khushchev himself assumed
overall responsibility for this aspect of the apparatus, for no other

major Party figure dealt extensively with these questions. The two specialized agencies continued, however, to operate as they had before the war. As noted above, Zlenko continued to direct the organization-instruction section until 1947.[7]

Spivak was replaced as cadres secretary by another major official of the Ukrainian apparatus, Alesksei Alekseevich Epishev, previously first secretary of Kharkov obkom. Epishev held the post until late 1948, when the entire staff agency system was drastically revised. Both the organizational and personnel branches were dissolved and replaced, as far as "internal" Party duties were concerned, by the Party-Trade Union-Komsomol Organizations Section (later called simply the Party Organizations Section). Staff functions in state and economic institutions were once again delegated to the Party "industrial" sections or to the state and economic institutions themselves. These organizational changes came at a time when the apparatus was relatively stable compared to the periods immediately preceding and following the war. By 1950 only 1,500 Party and state officials had been removed for inefficiency; by 1954 fewer had been dismissed in the entire Ukraine than had been removed in Stalino oblast alone during the first year after the Soviet reconquest.[8] These changed circumstances doubtless reduced to some extent the importance of the staff sections. Nevertheless, it is evident that the personnel of the Party Organizations Section ensures a considerable measure of continuity with the earlier staff agencies. For example, of three deputy directors reported, one had formerly headed an obkom organizational-instruction section, and another had been deputy director of the cadres section.

Continuity of personnel, in spite of the formal changes in the structure of the staff agencies, was still more evident at the lower levels of the apparatus. Both during Burmistenko's ascendancy and after the war, many second secretaries acted as general directors and coordinators of staff activities. At times there was almost a formal recognition of this relationship; for example, in 1946 a seminar on Party structure and similar questions was specifically designated for the categories of second secretaries and cadres secretaries of the raikoms. Since the abolition of the organization-instruction and the cadres sections a number of obkom second secretaries have continued to deliver the principal reports on both cadres and organizational work and have been treated by other speakers in Party conferences as the persons principally responsible for these aspects of Party work.[9] On the other hand, in about half of the obkoms the second secretary has not supervised staff functions, which are then usually left to the first secretary. The division of responsibility between the chief of the oblast party organization and his first lieutenant seems, therefore, to be an *ad hoc* one, depending on the relative importance of the task at various times and places and on the backgrounds of the two secretaries.

An additional factor of continuity in staff operation at the oblast level has been provided by the obkom cadres secretary. While the position of cadres secretary was abolished in 1948 along with the cadres section itself, the individuals who had held these posts generally continued for a time to be obkom secretaries (listed fourth or fifth in the group) and evidently maintained some responsibility for personnel supervision.

The continuity in direction of personnel operations arising from the continued concern of individual officials with this function has inevitably diminished with the passage of time and the replacement of the individuals involved. Personnel supervision, formally divided among the Party organs sections and the "industrial" sections, is nominally coordinated only by the bureau of the obkom or its secretariat. There is a strong suggestion, however, that the key figures are the *nomenklatura* officials, those directly engaged in keeping personnel records, analyzing performance, and recommending assignments. "*Nomenklatura* workers are very important, enabling the directing party organs to keep the principal posts in their hands, to study the cadres, to choose and distribute them."[10] Apparently many of the *nomenklatura* officials, who once formed a key "sector" of the cadres section, have been reassigned to the new sections concerned with personnel. Unfortunately, the relatively low position of these officials makes it impossible to trace their individual assignments in the press. Possibly, however, some of these work directly under the obkom secretary most concerned with organizational matters. In any case, this secretary—whether the second secretary or another—evidently maintains a special relation to *nomenklatura* officials throughout the obkom apparatus. Thus an institutional feature of considerable importance continues to provide a measure of unity in cadres operations.

Since the cadres secretary occupied a relatively low position in the obkom hierarchy, information concerning him is comparatively scanty. While most of the eight whose previous careers can be traced were in such apparatus jobs as deputy director of an obkom cadres section, director of an organization-instruction section, and Komsomol secretary, two were in Party posts primarily concerned with economic direction.

An examination of the subsequent posts held by the fifteen for whom information of this type is available provides additional evidence of the variety of career experiences of cadres secretaries. Five became second secretaries of the obkoms in which they had directed the cadres section. In all likelihood this promotion represented in part a continuation of their duties of supervising personnel work. In most instances the promotion came before the abolition of the cadres secretaryship, however; consequently, it was not simply a device to circumvent the formal abolition of the cadres post.

Two of the cadres secretaries were transferred in grade to other obkoms. For officials in cadres work, however, such inter-oblast transfers appear to have been exceptional. As noted above, only two cadres secretaries were transferred to other oblasts when promoted, while all eight of those whose previous careers can be traced had worked in the same oblast in which they became cadres secretary. On the whole, cadres officials appear to have been persons who frequently transferred to other types of Party or Soviet work, but who usually remained for considerable parts of their careers in the same oblast.

Compared to the cadres secretary, the director of the obkom organization-instruction section was of relatively minor importance in the oblast Party hierarchy. Apparently he was never a member of the obkom bureau, and he is rarely noticed in the Republic press. Consequently, it is even more difficult to trace his career than it is that of the cadres secretary. The few instances available suggest that an organization-instruction director, like the cadres secretary, tended to remain in the same oblast when transferred. As in the case of the cadres official, there are instances (possibly less common) of transfer to line posts; two directors became second secretaries, one a gorkom secretary, and one a cadres secretary.

As noted in Chapter 4, all types of officials of the staff agencies receive their training in the general courses of the Party schools. Consequently, in spite of their specialist role at an early stage of their Party careers, the staff officials do not form a distinct group, but are intermingled with the generalists. In their day-to-day activities the staff specialists also work closely with the line officials. As previously noted, the technical aspects of personnel selection, for example, are decided by the cadres officials, but the responsibility for appointments is formally in the hands of the Party committee and actually rests with its first or its second secretary. If even higher-level cadres officials select men without taking into account the wishes of the Party committees under which the new appointees are to work, they are sharply criticized, as was the Rovno Party apparatus because:

> . . . the oblast organizations frequently selected directing Party cadres without appraisal of the political and business qualities of the workers and sent them to work at times without taking into account the opinions of the raikoms.[11]

More generally, however, the tendency of the cadres officials appears to be to defer to the wishes of the more powerful line officials. The L'vov Party organizations, which were "extraordinarily slow in overcoming mistakes in the selection of cadres,"[12] have been singled out for criticism in this regard;

> The practice of selection of cadres is at times completely irresponsible. The bureau of the [L'vov] gorkom, for example, appointed as Party organizer of a factory the worker of the Party gorkom, Comrade Varich. After four months, without changing the first recommendation, the bureau recommended for the very same work a second worker, Comrade Oparin. Comrade Valiuko, the instructor of the cadres section who

prepared the matter of Oparin, declared in the cadres section: "I do not know Comrade Oparin, but the secretary of the raikom, Comrade Sheremet'ev, recommended him; therefore it should be concurred in."

Without even having seen Comrade Oparin and without having talked with him, the instructor of the gorkom reported to the bureau the "data" he had concerning him, and the bureau stamped its approval on the proposal of the instructor.[13]

If the cadres officials are brought into frequent contact with the line group, this is necessarily still more true of the organization-instruction officials, a large part of whose work consists in providing technical advice and inspecting the operations of line officials. A major portion of this contact takes place in the "cabinets" or offices of the city Party committees. A major function of the cabinet is to act as a point for collection and analysis of a wide variety of material, including data on the organization of local Party branches and those in other parts of the U.S.S.R. On the basis of this material the Party officials—particularly the directors and instructors of the Party organizations section of the gorkom—relate general principles of Party work to the conditions and experience in their own areas.

The final stage of the work centered around the cabinet is the instruction of the raikom and other officials in improvement of organizational work. Among the subjects covered in one major city were: the holding of Party meetings (including the form of the minutes), the maintenance of Party accounts, the implementation of Party decisions, and the direction of trade union and Komsomol organization. The instructional staff was built around the director of the Party organizations section, his two deputies, and the section instructors, but it enlisted the assistance of the gorkom secretaries and directors of other sections, as well as urban raikom secretaries for special assignments.[14] Moreover, according to Soviet analysts, the seminars conducted in the cabinets occupy a key position in training lower Party officials in proper organization of the apparatus.[15]

The instructors, in even closer contact with the line officials than are the directing officials of the cabinets, comprised a ma-

jority of the rank-and-file officials of the organization-instruction
sections and were an important element of the cadres sections
before 1948. Instructors have continued to constitute a principal
body of officials in the Party organizations sections, and they are
also assigned to the "industrial branch" sections. In all cases,
their tasks have been much the same: day-to-day checking on the
operation of lower Party organizations, insurance that the various
Party sections adhered to their prescribed spheres of operation, instruction of officials in proper methods of Party operation, and, in
general, seeing that orders from higher authorities are implemented:

> The instructor is a salient figure of the Party apparatus. To
> a great extent the style of work of Party organs depends on
> the manner in which the instructor works, in which he carries
> out his immediate tasks.[16]

In carrying out these very difficult and delicate tasks, the instructor has been hampered by the fact that he is himself a relatively unimportant official. While this post is occasionally a
stepping-stone to prominence, an even higher proportion of instructors than of raikom secretaries seems to fall by the wayside.
Moreover, in spite of the fact that the position of the obkom instructor makes it desirable, according to a Soviet writer, that
he "stand on the level" of the raikom secretary,[17] the instructor,
unlike the secretary, is rarely a member of the obkom itself. The
instructor is therefore at a disadvantage in dealing with the line
officials whose mistakes he must correct. He is supposed to work
intimately with these more powerful figures, yet to maintain his
role as a liaison officer and as a representative of higher authority.
The line officials, on the other hand, evidently endeavor to divert
the instructor from this function, which might be embarrassing
to them, and to use him for purposes which redound to their own
advantage.

> The instructor must be able to spend a large portion of his
> time in the primary Party organizations, to acquaint himself
> with the state of Party life on the spot, and to help the primary
> Party organizations to organize Party-political work well. It is
> inadmissible that instructors should be unable to make the

most of their assignments and at the same time be prevented
from successfully carrying out their role as connecting links
between the directing Party organs and the primary Party
organizations . . . .

But in some organizations matters go to the other extreme.

The director of the organization-instruction section of the
Tiligul-Berezanka raikom of the KP(b)U (Nikolaev oblast)
and the instructors of the section are assigned most of the time
to specific kolkhozes. As a result, they do not go to the primary Party organizations and do not occupy themselves with
matters of Party-organizational work.[18]

Apparently this diversion of the instructor from his proper
functional activity became more frequent—as might have been
anticipated—when the organization-instruction section was dissolved and the instructors were placed under Party sections directly concerned with economic production. Seven years after
the warning just quoted, a front-page editorial in *Pravda Ukrainy*
criticized the following situation:

> In a number of rural raikoms of the Party instructors are being
> used as permanent plenipotentiaries for various activities in
> the kolkhozes. Thus, in Glinsk raion, Sumy oblast, the in-
> structors of the raikom of the KP(b)U have been sitting for
> months without interruption in the kolkhozes to which they
> have been attached, occupied with economic affairs and un-
> able to devote serious attention to other matters . . . .
>
> Regardless of which section of the Party committee the in-
> structor works in, and to which area he is assigned, he must
> enter deeply into Party life. The instructor must interest him-
> self in how Party decisions and directives are fulfilled, raise
> by all means possible the level of organizational and mass
> political work of Party organizations, and develop criticism
> and self-criticism . . . .
>
> The duty of the instructor is **to** study and generalize the ex-
> perience of Party work, to raise new questions of vital im-
> portance for decision by the bureau of the Party committee.[19]

While in the cases just noted the Republic staff authorities objected to the diversion of the lower-level staff officials from their
assigned tasks, there is significantly no assertion that the staff

officials concerned objected, or even that their immediate superiors in charge of the raikom or obkom staff agencies protested.

The tendency for solidarity, rather than divergence of interest, to develop among staff and line officials in a given area sometimes proceeds so far as to negate the function of the staff agencies as the "eyes" of higher authority. The most common manifestation of this tendency is the formation of "family groups" among officials in a given territory—overt or tacit agreements to protect the members from outside criticism and to see that they are provided with attractive positions. For example, it is asserted that the L'vov oblast agricultural department was so infested with "family groups" that a man who had been convicted for malfeasance in office, who was expelled from the Party, and who falsely claimed to have advanced agricultural training was retained as director of the livestock section for a considerable period.[20]

Similarly, in L'vov city in 1947, the first secretary, the secretary for cadres, and other officials, "created for themselves a familial atmosphere in the apparatus, employing every means to see that their dirty linen was not washed in public." The revelation of this state of affairs came, apparently, not from the heads of the staff sections, who were in collusion with the line secretaries, but from minor staff officials. When an instructor criticized the cadres officials for placing speculators in posts in the trade organization, the first secretary, Ivan Ivanovich Bondar', denounced him for "compromising" the gorkom.[21] Apparently these arrangements, however injurious to the interests of the Party as a whole, have not usually resulted from efforts of the line Party officials to override the cadres specialists, but have been the result of amicable connivance between the latter and their superiors in line functions.

The existence of specialized functional agencies for supervising the work of subordinate organizations and the flow of personnel are essential to the maintenance of any system in which authority is highly centralized. In particular, a system such as the Soviet, which is ruled by an "artificial elite" composed of persons selected and "developed" by the regime itself, is largely dependent on the mechanisms of cadres management for its successful functioning. The importance attached throughout the period studied to the

question of cadres selection and development testifies to the recognition of this fact by the Communist rulers in the Ukraine.

In view of this circumstance, it is somewhat surprising that the
cadres and organizational branches of the apparatus have not had
a more autonomous position. Here, if anywhere in the Party system, one might expect to find an "inner elite" distinguished from
other Party officials by recruitment, training, and career.

It is, perhaps, of secondary importance that the formal mechanisms for carrying on cadres and organizational work have frequently changed. There has been, as shown above, a fair degree
of continuity of function and personnel in spite of the structural
changes. Nevertheless, the mere fact that these agencies could be
shuffled so readily indicates that they can scarcely constitute the
citadels of an unassailable inner elite. Moreover, the transfer of
the major portion of their non-Party functions to state and economic
organizations, in spite of the continued general predominance
of the Party in all phases of Soviet life, suggests that the staff mechanisms occupy a relatively minor position in the total power picture.[22]

Of more significance, however, is the position of the cadres
and organizational specialists themselves. As individuals, their
chances of advancement are relatively good. Many move to second
secretaryships; this post may even be regarded in considerable
measure as the "natural" promotion for these specialists. At that
level the official has already ceased to be a staff specialist and has
entered the main operating sphere of Party leadership, even though
his major responsiblity may continue to be overseeing internal
Party affairs. From the second secretaryship to the position of
first secretary ("boss" of the region) is a relatively short step.
The most prominent example of such advancement is Leonti
Ivanovich Naidek, who served as secretary for cadres of the Odessa
obkom before the war, as second secretary of the same obkom
during and immediately after hostilities, as first secretary successively of the Kirovograd and the Odessa obkoms (1952-1957),
and most recently as second secretary of the KPU.

The very fact that the prospects of promotion are good would
seem likely to develop in the staff specialist a feeling that he has
a greater stake in the line aspects of the Party system than in the

staff. Moreover, the functional specialist's sense of solidarity with the top territorial officials is probably considerably enhanced by the fact that he often spends much of his career in a single territorial division. Moving from post to post within the same oblast, he can scarcely fail to develop a certain amount of fellow-feeling with other officials in the area, perhaps even that feeling of "local patriotism" which leads Party officials to endeavor to conceal the faults and the self-seeking of their associates from higher authorities. While the direct evidence available is far from conclusive on this point, the few examples available tend to support deductions drawn from this consideration of the nature of the specialist's career pattern.

One may well ask why the Communist Party, so intent on avoiding regional autonomy in its ranks and so vigorous in maintaining checks and informers on local officials, has permitted such a situation to develop. Naturally, any reasons advanced must be highly speculative. One possible reason is the possession by the Party of numerous alternative mechanisms for preventing the feeling of regional solidarity from proceeding too far. A possible secondary consideration is the need for allowing considerable leeway to top obkom officials in finding personnel and in carrying on organizational work during the period of heavy demands upon the Party.

Probably the most important influences were of a personal nature. While Burmistenko guided both cadres and organizational functions, his powerful position and exercise of close supervision probably stifled any tendency to regional solidarity. His sudden removal from the scene must have considerably weakened the central staff mechanism. While other types of Party leaders held the foreground in Kiev, secondary figures directed the cadres and organizational sections. Since then staff agencies, while important, have definitely been of an instrumental rather than of a directing nature.

Footnotes to Chapter 6

[1.] In addition to the agencies of the secretariats discussed in this chapter, there are certain special bodies which also perform staff tasks. The Organizational Bureau (Orgburo), a junior and more specialized counterpart of the Politburo, existed until 1952. Similarly, the Central Auditing Commission, a kind of junior Central Committee elected at each Congress, supervises Party finances. The Party Commission (for a time known as the Party College) reviews Party operations, especially expulsion or other punishment of members. The permanent personnel of all these agencies appears to be frequently interchanged with the secretariat staff agencies.

[2.] *KPSU v resoliutsiiakh i resheniakh s"ezdov, konferentsii i plenumov TsK* [The CPSU in Resolutions and Decisions of the Congresses, Conferences, and Plenums of the Central Committee] [Moscow: Gosudarstvennoe Izdatel'stvo Politicheskoi Literatury, 1953), II, 919-920.

[3.] A. Fedorov, *The Underground Committee Carries On* (Moscow: Foreign Languages Publishing House, 1952), p. 16; Aleksandr Nikolaevich Saburov, *Za liniieiu frontu* [Behind the Front Line] (L'vov: Knyzhkovo-Zhurnal'ne Vydavnytsvo, 1953), p. 12.

[4.] See an account of the interrogation of a captured Soviet officer of the Ukrainian Staff of the partisan movement, Aleksandr Ruzanov, contained in *Krakivs'ki Visti* (a Ukrainian nationalist paper published under German occupation), October 23, 1943 (hereafter cited as "Ruzanov"). Since Ruzanov was a prisoner of the Nazis when he made his statement concerning Spivak's nationality, it might be regarded as suspect but for the secretary's first name, Moisei—sometimes listed as Musii (*Visti*, June 29, 1938), a name rarely held in Russia or in the Ukraine by a non-Jew. As late as February, 1939, just before the creation of the cadres secretaryship, Spivak was only third secretary of the Kiev obkom (*Pravda*, February 9, 1939).

[5.] On Spivak's role in the partisan movement, see Ruzanov; also see Fedorov, p. 510.

[6.] Inspectors of the Central Committee of the KPU are fairly important officials, apparently with roving commissions to keep the Republic Party authorities informed on Party operations in outlying areas. It is not clear whether they are responsible to some section of the Secretariat or whether they report directly to the principal secretaries or to the Presidium (Politburo) as a whole.

[7.] At that time this section was replaced by the Administration for Verification of Party Organs, headed by Sergei Iakovlevich Vaksman. See *Pravda*, January 26, 1949.

[8.] I. T. Pinegin, "Rabota KP Ukrainy po osushchestvleniiu reshenii partii o podbore, rasstanovke i vospitanii rukovodiashchikh partiinykh i sovetskikh kadrov v poslevoennyi period (1946-1955 gg.)" [The Work of the Communist Party of the Ukraine in Carrying Out the Decisions of the Party Concerning the Selection, Assignment, and Training of Directing Party and Soviet Cadres in the Postwar Period (1946-1955)], an unpublished dissertation for obtaining the academic degree of candidate of historical sciences in the Academy of Social Sciences of the Central Committee of the CPSU, Moscow, 1955, p. 95.

[9.] Cf. especially the role of Vladimir Vladimirovich Skriabin, the second

86   *The Soviet Bureaucratic Elite*

secretary of Dnepropetrovsk obkom, as shown in the obkom plenum reported in *PU*, May 12, 1953, and in the oblast Party conference, *PU*, February 15, 1951. See also the discussion by A. I. Ustenko, second secretary of Kamenets-Podolsk obkom, *PU*, July 30, 1952; and G. G. Petrov, second secretary of Kirovograd obkom, *PU*, January 5, 1949.

10. L. Slepov, *Mestnye partiinye organy: Lektsii prochitannye v Vyshei Partiinoi Shkole pri TsK KPSS, Kafedra Partiinogo Stroitel'stva* [Local Party Organs: Lectures Delivered in the Higher Party School of the Central Committee of the CPSU, Department of Party Structure] (Moscow: Vyshaia Partiinaia Shkola pri TsK KPSS, 1954), p. 52.

11. *PU*, August 5, 1952.

12. M. D. Likhenko, "Bor'ba kommunisticheskoi partii Sovetskogo Soiuza za ideino-politicheskoe vospitanie rukovodiashchikh partiinykh i sovetiskih kadrov (1946-1950 gg.). Na materialiakh Ukrainy [The Struggle of the Communist Party of the Soviet Union for Idea-Political Education of Directing Party and Soviet Cadres (1946-1950). From Materials of the Ukraine], an unpublished dissertation for obtaining the academic degree of candidate of historical sciences in the Institute for Improving the Qualifications of Teachers of Marxism-Leninism, Kiev State University, 1955, p. 101.

13. "Kak podbiraiut i vospityaiut kadry vo L'vove" [How Cadres are Selected and Trained in L'vov], *PU*, July 6, 1946.

14. I. Kalinichenko, director of the Party trade-union-Komsomol organizations section of L'vov gorkom, "Kabinet organizatsionno-partiinoi raboty" [The Cabinet of Party Organizational Work], *PU*, October 19, 1949. Cf. G. Shumskii, secretary of Oktiabr (Kharkov city) raikom, "Napolehlyvo pratsiuvaty z novoobranymy sekretariamy" [Work Perseveringly With the Newly-Elected Secretaries]. *RU*, March 16, 1952, and A. Lisovin, *Biblioteka gorkoma partii* [The Library of the Gorkom of the Party] (Moscow: Gospolitizdat, 1955).

15. V. I. Zhadovets, "Deiatel'nost' kommunisticheskoi partii v oblasti dal'neishego ukrepleniia sovetskogo gosudarstvennogo apparata v gody chetvertoi piatiletki (na materialiakh Ukrainskoi S.S.R.)" [The Activity of the Communist Party in the Area of Further Strengthening the Soviet State Apparatus During the Years of the Fourth Five-Year Plan. (From Materials of the Ukrainian S.S.R.)], an unpublished dissertation for obtaining the academic degree of candidate of historical sciences in the Institute for Improving the Qualifications of Teachers of Marxism-Leninism, Kiev University, 1956, pp. 108-109.

16. Viktor I. Alidin, deputy director of the Organization-Instruction Section of the Central Committee, "Deiaki pytannia roboty partiinoho aparatu" [Some Questions on the Work of the Party Apparatus], *RU*, August 25, 1945. Cf. Slepov, p. 56.

17. Slepov, p. 58.

18. Alidin in *RU*, August 25, 1945.

19. "Instruktor partiinogo komiteta" [The Instructor of the Party Committee], *PU*, July 15, 1952.

20. Report of obkom first secretary, M. Lazurenko, *PU*, May 12, 1953. Cf. Grigori Ivanovich Kulik, "Ukraïns'ki burzhuazni natsionalisty—liuti vorohy trudiashchykh" [The Ukrainian Bourgeois Nationalists—Fierce Enemies of the Toilers], an unpublished dissertation for obtaining the academic degree

of candidate of historical sciences in the Kiev State University, 1947, p. 242.

[21.] According to an article by four instructors of the obkom, "Nepravyl'ne stavlennia l'vivs'koho mis'kkomu KP(b)U do doboru i vykhovannia kadriv" [The Incorrect Position of the L'vov Gorkom of the KP(b)U on the Selection and Training of Cadres], *RU*, February 16, 1947.

[22.] On this general point, see the similar conclusions reached by Louis Nemzer, "The Kremlin's Professional Staff; The 'Apparatus' of the Central Committee, Communist Party of the Soviet Union," *American Political Science Review*, XLIV (March, 1950), pp. 64-85.

7

Indoctrination Specialists

Iᴛ is scarcely an exaggeration to say that the Soviet system rests upon indoctrination. Termed "ideological work" by Soviet writers, indoctrination means, of course, the process of securing the internal consent of the population to the current policies and interpretations of events presented by the leadership, as well as its allegiance to the ideology generally referred to as "Marxism-Leninism." Despite their frequent resort to extreme coercion to secure external compliance with their commands, the Soviet leaders have realized that the system can be stable only if the mass of the people is at least half-convinced of the wisdom of these commands and of the ideology underlying them.

Because the process of indoctrination is essentially political, it has been reserved almost entirely to the Party itself.[1] Since securing the loyalty of the population is central to the aims of the regime, the major leaders of the Party at each level of its structure devote a great deal of attention to this activity. In the Ukraine the first secretaries usually devote a considerable proportion of their reports to Congresses and other general speeches to indoctrinational matters, and the reports of the obkom first secretaries follow a similar pattern. Frequently, too, the second secretaries at both the Central Committee and the obkom level have devoted a great deal of attention to indoctrination.

In addition to being of central interest to these line officials at each level of the Party, however, the indoctrinational field is the special province of a highly ramified branch of the Party organization. The central agency of this network is the Propaganda and Agitation Section of the Central Committee Secretariat, with corresponding sections at the lower levels of the Party pyramid.[2] While there have been several changes in the scope and organization of the propaganda and agitation sections, they have been a constant feature of the Party organization.

It is true that the office of "secretary of propaganda" of the obkom, which was established in 1939, was abolished in 1948. In a large majority of the obkoms, however, the individual who had acted as propaganda secretary was simply redesignated "secretary of the obkom" (he was usually listed fourth or fifth among the secretaries) and continued to supervise indoctrination. While there have naturally been a large number of changes in these posts since 1948, one obkom secretary appears always to be a propaganda specialist. Consequently, it appears appropriate to refer to this group from 1938 to the present as the "obkom propaganda secretaries."

Since the propaganda secretary occupies a relatively low place in the obkom apparatus, published references to him are much rarer than are those concerning the first secretary. As a result, precise statistical data concerning the occupants of this post are unobtainable. The fragmentary data available suggests, however, that the propaganda secretary spends on the average about the same time in office as does the first secretary—three years. The propaganda secretary is also transferred in grade about as frequently as is the first secretary; of the twenty-seven (less than one-third of the total number) whose careers could be traced in some detail, eleven were transferred to the same post in a different obkom. It is important to note, however, that the propaganda secretary was not, as a rule, transferred to the same oblast as was the first secretary under whom he had served; nor did his period in office usually coincide with that of the first secretary, although it was of about the same length.

An examination of the sparse information available concerning the earlier careers of individuals who became propaganda secretaries suggests further divergences from the career pattern of the first secretary outlined earlier. An outstanding feature is the propaganda secretary's tendency to have a background of earlier posts in the indoctrinational field. Of eight individuals whose careers could be traced, five had been directors or deputy directors of obkom propaganda sections—i.e., had held a post immediately below that of propaganda secretary.[3] One had edited an oblast newspaper, another had edited *Partiine Zhittia*, a Party ideological journal. The remaining two had been first secretaries of urban raions (wards) in Kiev. Normally, these would be considered "line" or generalist posts, but accounts of the activities of these secretaries in raions which contained numerous institutions heavily engaged in ideological work suggest that their duties may have resembled those of the indoctrination specialist rather than the typical first secretary.

The career of Mariia Maksimovna Pidtychenko provides a somewhat more concrete picture of the ladder which an obkom propaganda secretary may ascend.[4] In passing, it is worth noting that women, while only a small minority among indoctrination officials, are considerably more heavily represented in this branch of Party activity, involving primarily verbal skills, than in aspects which call for managerial activity. It seems also to be rather typical that Madame Pidtychenko should have started her climb as an apparatus official after she had already entered the teaching profession. In 1939, while serving as instructor of a chemical technological institute in Dnepropetrovsk, she was elected secretary for propaganda of the oblast Communist Youth League (the Komsomol indoctrinational organization mirrors that of the Party and is a frequent source of recruits for the senior indoctrinational machine). A year later Madame Pidtychenko became secretary of the Central Committee of Komsomols. After a period of indoctrination work among Ukrainian youths who were evacuated to Ufa during the war, she returned to the Ukraine as secretary for propaganda of the Kiev gorkom. In this key post of the indoctrinational network she evidently enjoyed the special confidence of major Party leaders. This is indicated by the suggestion of drastic changes in Party educational requirements which she made at the Seventeenth Congress and also by the fact that she was sent to Scotland on a mission of "trade union" delegates as early as 1951, when only the most reliable Soviet citizens were allowed abroad.

A major aspect of the propaganda sections' work is the direction of oral "propaganda and agitation."[5] From the point of view of the apparatus, this aspect of its work is doubly important because the large number of persons engaged in it provides an ample field for recruitment of professional indoctrination personnel. While Soviet Communism has constantly stressed oral indoctrination, it has not neglected mass media of communication. These, too, are under the supervision of the propaganda and agitation sections. Formally, radio (and probably television, now operating in Kiev) is directed by a committee of the Council of Ministers. The close connection of this committee to the indoctrinational machine is suggested by the fact that it was headed by the former deputy director of the Komsomol Central Committee Agitation and Propaganda Section.[6] Occasionally radio has been used as an adjunct to Party indoctrination courses, but little use of the medium for avowed indoctrination purposes has been reported.[7] Similarly, the pervasive indoctrinational content of motion pictures tends to be concealed rather than explicit. Motion picture production is also organized under an agency of the Council of Ministers, but again, significantly, the director has been a former propaganda secretary.[8]

Compared to the printed word, however, other media of mass communication receive relatively little stress in the U.S.S.R. The role of *Pravda* and of other publications in the revolutionary struggle has covered the entire press with reflected glory. At an early date the most prominent Bolshevik leaders adopted the practice of contributing to the Party press and of even acting as editors; this practice, continued to the present time, has increased the prestige of the newspaper. Moreover, the printed page—especially in newspaper form—is especially adaptable to Soviet propaganda requirements: it can be distributed widely, yet it can be subjected to strict supervision before issuance. It provides the principal source of information on Party policy and interpretation of current events in a form which, unlike the radio or motion picture, can be easily preserved and utilized by the propaganda specialist as a source for his talks.

The factors just mentioned have given the newspaper a role in the Ukrainian indoctrination network second only to that of the oral indoctrination machine. Among newspapers outside Kiev those in the Ukrainian language predominate, although about ten of the larger oblasts have Russian-language newspapers as well, and in the West Ukraine there are several in minority languages. Nationality background apparently has little, if any, effect on the careers of individual editors, however. For example, a woman, Raisa Iukhimovna Khomiakova, probably Jewish, successively edited the Russian-language and Ukrainian-language papers of Dnepropetrovsk, serving in between as director of the obkom propaganda and agitation section.

Both factors prominent in the instance just considered—absence of nationality qualification and intimate interrelationship between journalism and direction of propaganda activities—are illustrated in the careers of the editors of the Republic newspapers. One editor of *Pravda Ukrainy*, a Russian-language paper, had previously edited the Ukrainian-language newspaper of Stalino oblast. Another, Lev Israelevich Troskunov, was apparently Jewish. The present editor, Nikolai Kondratevich Belogurov, was successively editor of the Kharkov oblast Ukrainian-language paper, propaganda secretary of Kharkov obkom, director of the Propaganda and Agitation Section of the Central Committee Secretariat, and director of its Belletristic and Art Affairs Section.

The pattern of transfer of editors to the most varied types of work in the indoctrination field is still better illustrated by the careers of the editors of the Republic Ukrainian-language paper.[9] The prewar editor, Andrei Terenteiovich Chekaniuk, was later deputy director of the Propaganda and Agitation Administration of the Central Committee Secretariat, then, as previously noted, rector of the Higher Party School. His postwar successor, Luka Fomich Palamarchuk, became Ukrainian Minister of Foreign Affairs—a post which is obviously more important for propaganda activities (especially in the United Nations) than for normal diplomacy.

While the Republic and oblast newspaper editors can be assumed to be reliable and well-trained, as well as influential, the supply of competent journalists in the Ukraine has been distinctly limited. Recently a faculty of journalism was established at Kiev University, and it has now begun to supply specialists for the raion press.[10] During most of the postwar period, however, only two Party institutions, both under direct Party control, have provided journalistic training. The division of journalism of the Kharkov oblast Party school, successor to the Kharkov Communist Institute of Journalism, one of the oldest Soviet training centers for newspaper work, enrolled 150 in 1951, an increase of only ten per cent over the immediate postwar period.[11] The journalism section of the Higher Party School in Kiev, opened in 1946, had only seventy-five enrollees.[12] There are over 1,100 newspapers in the Ukraine. Even taking into account the fact that the vast majority are in raions, small cities, or factories, and that these have staffs of two to four writers, it is evident that the yearly need for replacements can scarcely be met by the graduates of the institutions just mentioned. While the universities train some journalists, it appears that they receive newspaper posts of lesser importance from the political standpoint.

There is some evidence that even the training given in the specialized institutions, both Party and university, is defective.[13] In 1951 a student at the Kharkov school complained that the journalism section did not form a separate department but was under the Department of Marxism-Leninism, whose director showed little interest in preparing journalists. The reading room for journalism students was rarely open and, in any case, contained nothing but "ordinary" diagrams and a few files of local newspapers. The school library had few books and pamphlets on journalism. Although the students had proposed the formation of groups to study stenography and photography and although they wished to have sessions with experienced journalists, nothing had been done. At one point the press sector of the obkom propaganda and agitation section gave each student an assignment to write a survey of the city and raion newspapers but failed to provide sufficient instructions or to criticize the papers submitted.[14] If this picture is at all typical, it—together with the shortage of trained journalists—goes far toward explaining the numerous deficiencies of the Ukrainian press which are obvious to the outside observer and which are, indeed, frequently criticized by Communist sources. It may also help to explain why a considerable number of the lower-level personnel of the newspaper staffs defected to the Ukrainian nationalist groups during the war or collaborated with the German occupation forces.[15]

The newspaper is by far the most important printed vehicle of indoctrination. The propaganda and agitation sections have, however, general oversight over all publications, even those which are ostensibly purely cultural. At the oblast level this supervision is formalized through the appointment of the propaganda secretary— or his subordinate—to the editorial boards of periodicals.[16] Occasionally at the Republic level more direct measures have been taken to secure conformity to Party wishes. This seems to have been particularly true during the campaign for ideological "purity" conducted by Andrei Zhdanov in 1946. At that time the editor of *Vitchysna* (Fatherland), organ of the Union of Soviet Writers of the Ukraine, was denounced as a propagandist of "bourgeois nationalists" and replaced by the assistant director of the Propaganda and Agitation Administration itself.[17] Almost simultaneously the editor of the humor magazine *Perets* (Pepper), who was accused of failure to satirize the foreign and domestic foes of the regime, was replaced by the former editor of the L'vov oblast Komsomol newspaper.[18]

More recently, direction of literary publications has been assigned to various sections of the Central Committee Secretariat, organizationally distinct from the Agitation and Propaganda Section but closely connected to it through their personnel. The assignment of N. K. Belogurov to the directorship of the Belletristic and Art Affairs Section after a long career as editor and propaganda director has already been noted; another former propaganda director became Director of the Cultural and Scientific Section. A similar situation exists in the agencies of the Council of Ministers concerned with propaganda or cultural matters. In addition to the Ministry of Foreign Affairs, RATAU (Radio-Telegraphic Agency of the Ukraine, the official news agency) and the Committee on Art Affairs have been directed by former propaganda officials.

The picture just presented is one of a widely ramified and changing network of opinion-forming organizations, linked by a frequent interchange of directing personnel, and subject to the overall supervision of the propaganda sections. The indoctrination field is also integrated by the common background of training of its personnel. As noted in an earlier chapter, Party schools are under the direct supervision of the propaganda sections, and directors and many of the instructional staff are persons who have worked in general indoctrinational activities. Within these schools propagandists and journalists follow training courses which have much in common but which are distinct from the courses pursued by other groups of Party officials.[19] In addition, the propaganda sections carry on very extensive programs of on-the-job training for their own personnel. The propaganda sections try hard to relate this training as intimately as possible to indoctrination work and to bring active propagandists together to discuss their problems and analyze their experiences:

> Propaganda work in itself is the best stimulus for the ideological growth of the cadres. In our practice we try to create an atmosphere of exactingness toward the propagandist in the Party organization; in this way he is compelled to do a great deal of reading, to follow current events, to study his own experience and that of his comrades, and to carry on propaganda at a high level of ideas.[20]

For a time the principal instrument of training at the local level was the propaganda seminar, at which officials presented analyses of their indoctrinal work in varied environments[21]. More recently the seminar, which met only a few times a month, has been criticized as "episodic," and it has been replaced—in some areas at least—by systematic two-year courses in the Evening Universities of Marxism-Leninism. In addition to after-hours attendance, officials receive leave half a dozen times a year to attend special five-day sessions for discussion of theoretical questions and practical experience.[22]

Besides their primary function of providing training and of familiarizing indoctrinational workers with current Party policies and practices, these frequent assemblies seem likely to develop a sense of group solidarity. At a higher level, Republic and regional meetings of obkom propaganda secretaries, directors, and editors, with officials of the Central Committee Agitation and Propaganda Section, editors of Republic newspapers, and officials from the state agencies engaged in cultural and indoctrinational activities probably have the same effect.[23]

In contrast to the close contact of indoctrination officials with one another is their less intimate contact with other types of Party officials. As noted above, terms of obkom propaganda secretaries tend to overlap rather than to coincide with those of the first secretaries. This fact suggests that appointments of propaganda secretaries do not depend as a rule upon the wishes of the chief Party officials. No direct evidence on this point is available at the obkom level; formally, of course, all obkom secretaries are "elected" by the obkoms and confirmed by higher authorities. There is, however, one account of the process of appointment of a raikom propagandist. The candidate was recommended for the post by the raikom first secretary, whom he had known in the Army. Before the appointment was sent to the obkom for confirmation, however, the candidate was interviewed by the obkom propaganda secretary.[24] This suggests that, while many personal factors may enter into appointments, the propaganda officials have an important, if not a decisive, voice.

Officials in the indoctrination group are also clearly distinguished from other members of the Party apparatus by their career expectations. Line officials may reasonably anticipate transfer to many different types of Party work and even to State work. The indoctrination specialist may also look forward to a varied career, but very likely all his posts will lie in the propaganda, journalistic, and ideological fields. Of fifty-one officials in the indoctrination field whose careers could be followed in some detail, only seven were ever assigned posts which were not primarily concerned with such affairs. Of these seven, four became second secretaries, but, as noted earlier, the second secretary is often responsible for all aspects of "internal Party work." Consequently, the assumption of such a post meant at most a broadening of the indoctrination specialist's activities to include personnel and organizational functions, rather than an abandoning of propaganda tasks. It is also significant that none of these four second secretaries achieved the further promotion to first secretary, which would have brought them into broader managerial tasks, although such promotion is almost normal for second secretaries. The remaining four exceptions fall into no definite pattern, but in each case there is at least a suggestion that the "line" position assumed had an unusually important element of responsibility for indoctrination matters.

If, as the above evidence suggests, the indoctrinational career is a relatively "closed" one, one might expect solidarity of interest among its members to be reflected in certain attitudes of rivalry or friction toward other branches of the Party apparatus. Obviously, such evidence is very difficult to obtain, for such attitudes could not be expressed overtly within the monolithic Soviet system. Available indications are, moreover, complicated by other cross-currents, such as friction between oblast and Republic authorities. For example, V. S. Markov, a highly successful "line" secretary, strongly support-ed the propaganda and editorial officials of Odessa oblast in 1952 when he was first secretary there:

> ... [We] do not feel that we are getting the support we had hoped for from the sections of the KP(b)U of the Ukraine— propaganda and agitation, schools, literature and art. . . . . Undoubtedly the work of the oblast organizations has serious defects which it is necessary to criticize, and at the same time it is necessary to help them improve their work. The Republic papers *Radians'ka Ukraïna* and *Pravda Ukrainy* have published much critical material in their pages—accurate and useful. The local Party organizations are grateful for every critical article of the central [i.e., Moscow] and Republic newspapers which objectively reveals deficiencies in the work, as expressions of the anxiety of the Central Committee of the VKP(b) and the Central Committee of the KP(b)U to raise the level of Party, economic, and ideological work. But, unfortunately, insufficient feelings of responsibility on the part of individual workers of the newspapers lead to the appearance in their pages of articles which may confuse the readers and which are calculated only for external effect and not for serious help.[25]

Here the horizontal cleavage in the apparatus structure seems clear. In a number of instances, however, the propaganda section officials have come into direct conflict with line officials at the same territorial level. The newspaper is not permitted to oppose the directors of the Party organization to which it is attached.[26] On the other hand, the newspaper is officially permitted and urged to bring to light unsatisfactory conditions in its area. Since such conditions inevitably reflect upon the conduct of affairs by the line officials, they try to "shut up" the oblast or raion newspaper. For example, one raikom secretary took strong offense at the local paper's criticism of the raion agricultural instruction program, saying, "What kind of patriots of this raion are you, when you start writing things like that?"[27]

It is altogether natural that in such cases the higher-level papers should intervene, for a major function of the Soviet newspaper is to maintain a vigilant watch over local Party activities to prevent concealment of defects. It is significant that, in most cases reported, the various levels of the newspapers stand together against efforts of the line officials to stifle criticism. Moreover, there is more than a hint of resentment on the part of the journalists toward the overbearing attitude of line secretaries, and there is a good deal of scorn among the latter for the "seat-warmers" whose skills are verbal rather than operational. This comes out most clearly in newspaper reaction to what is apparently a prevalent practice of diversion of raion editorial writers to inspection or supervision of economic operations. The editor of *Radians'kyi Selianyn* (Soviet Villager) in Drogobych raion, for example, complained that the raikom secretary paid attention to the newspaper only when he needed "plenipotentiaries" to supervise agricultural work. The editor pointed out to the secretary that, since there were only two journalists on the staff, any such diversion of their efforts prevented efficient operation of the paper. When the journalist cited an article in the Moscow Party journal, *Kultura i Zhizn'* (Culture and Life), warning against such practices, the secretary scornfully replied, "I know these clever pieces; I can read the paper, too." He went on to indicate his low opinion of journalistic activities by refusing to let his subordinates contribute articles on rural life: "If the editors need material, let them go to the village and gather it themselves."[28]

A still more striking example of contemptuous treatment of the press by line officials occurred at a recent oblast Party conference in Rovno:

> . . . Aside from the editor of the oblast newspaper, Comrade Medianik, who was a delegate to the conference, not one worker of the oblast newspaper was invited to the conference. It is true that, after the persistent request of Comrade Medianik, the directors of the two basic sections of the editorial staff (the propaganda and the Party life) were admitted to the hall; but after the intermission the director of the special section of the

obkom, Comrade Kovtun, suggested that they leave the conference, as they were, he said, not delegates and not guests.[29]

If the indoctrinational group can occasionally express its resentment of line officials, it is nevertheless in a relatively weak position
in the apparatus as a whole. The relative weakness of the press is
suggested by the location of its principal Republic newspaper in a
rather cramped building in a quarter of Kiev remote from the im-
posing Party headquarters. The indoctrination specialists themselves
have been represented in the highest Party circles in the Ukraine,
but in relatively small numbers, and as a rule they have not attained the prominence accorded other major officials. Before the
war, the Secretary for Propaganda, I. G. Lysenko, received relatively little attention; his name was not mentioned after the outbreak
of hostilities.

Lysenko's successor, Konstantin Zakharovich Litvin, is a much
more influential figure. Once a Donbas laborer, his first important
post was that of official of a Party school in Stalino oblast. During
the war he continued his career in the Donbas, where he acted as
director of propaganda in Voroshilovgrad oblast. After serving as
Secretary for Propaganda in the Central Committee Secretariat
from 1944 to July, 1946, Litvin was promoted to third secretary.
In this position, the highest attained up to that time by an indoctrination specialist, he continued to be primarily concerned with
ideological and propaganda matters.

Litvin's promotion coincided with Andrei Zhdanov's intensive
campaign for complete ideological conformity in all aspects of
cultural life. Since a major role in this campaign was allotted to the
indoctrinational group, it rapidly increased in influence during 1946.
As late as March, 1946, at a Central Committee plenum discussion
of "internal Party work in Dnepropetrovsk, Poltava, and Drogobych
oblasts," the majority of participants were obkom first secretaries,
with only five of twenty-three speakers representing the indoctrination group.[30] Two months later, at a plenum discussion of "cultural-
educational work among factory workers in Voroshilovgrad, Mariupol', and villages of Nikolaev oblast," however, four members of the
Republic propaganda apparatus, five obkom propaganda secre-

taries, and a half-dozen other indoctrination workers formed the overwhelming majority of the participants.[31]

Zhdanov's eclipse and death in 1948 apparently did not result in any considerable diminution in importance of the indoctrination group. Litvin continued as one of the major figures of the Secretariat; in Central Committee plenums in 1948 and 1949, indoctrination officials continued to play the preponderant role in discussion of ideological and propaganda questions.

It seems possible that the "verbal specialists" had another, more subtle means of influence during this period. The proneness of powerful leaders in all modern countries to seek trusted assistants among opinion-moulding experts has often been noted. Apparently the Ukrainian Party leaders were no exception to this tendency. In 1948 P. N. Gapochka, who had been Khrushchev's aide during the war, became director of the Propaganda and Agitation Section. Khrushchev indicated his continued interest in Gapochka by interrupting the latter's address on indoctrinational matters to the Sixteenth Congress to pose a question.[32] About the same time, Sergei Grigorevich Segen became D. S. Korotchenko's counsellor when the latter was appointed Chairman of the Council of Ministers.[33] Like Gapochka, Segen had apparently been his chief's wartime aid (he had accompanied Korotchenko on inspection trips to partisan groups). Having edited the Komsomol paper, *Stalinskoe Plemia*, before the war, Segen also had a background as a propaganda specialist.

From 1950 on, the influence of the indoctrination group seems to have declined. In that year Litvin left the Secretariat to assume what was evidently a major post as Deputy Chairman of the Council of Ministers; not long afterwards, however, he was assigned the relatively obscure position of second secretary of L'vov obkom. Ivan Dmitreevich Nazarenko, who in 1946 had succeeded Litvin as secretary in charge of propaganda, continued to occupy a prominent position in top Party councils, but the representation of indoctrination officials in Central Committee sessions diminished. In June, 1950, only two of thirteen discussants of "Komosol work in politics and education" were indoctrination officials; in November, 1951, only eight of thirty-four speakers on "the improvement of ideological work" came from this group, while fifteen obkom first secretaries discussed the subject.[34]

It is worth noting that the decline in the relative prominence of the indoctrination group became apparent shortly after the departure of Nikita Khrushchev from the Ukraine at the end of 1949, though this may, of course, be sheer coincidence. It seemed that a low point in this process had been reached in June, 1953, when Litvin was dismissed from even his relatively low position in L'vov, and a great deal of criticism of "Russianization" of the western oblasts was directed at indoctrination activities. Litvin was restored to a relatively important position as Minister for Culture, and the indoctrination group as a whole seems to have increased somewhat in stature in subsequent years.

Early in July, 1956, Litvin was removed as Minister and assigned the relatively unimportant post of Chairman of the Ukrainian Society for Cultural Connections Abroad. His successor, Rotislav Vladimirovich Babiichuk, had been an inspector of the Central Committee and, earlier, an obkom secretary, but he had apparently not held an important post in propaganda work. Possibly of even greater significance was Nazarenko's resignation two weeks earlier. The Central Committee Secretary was said to be suffering from "a worsening state of health which could not be treated." His successor, Stephen Vasilovich Chervonenko, had attained a high post only two years earlier as Director of the Science and Culture Section of the Central Committee.

The available evidence strongly suggests that the body of indoctrination officials in the Ukraine is a relatively "closed" group with a considerable degree of group solidarity and special interest. In spite of the monolithic structure of the Party and the strong efforts of its leaders to prevent the formation of separate interest groups, the familiar cleavage between the man of words and the man of deeds seems to have developed. The great emphasis placed by the Soviet system upon rough-and-ready behavior and the tendency to fill top posts from "practical workers," especially those with technical training, have probably made the role of the ideological specialist a difficult one in many respects. Nevertheless, though the line official may scorn the specialist in verbal manipulation, he cannot carry on without him; nor can the indoctrination specialist, however much he may resent the line official's scorn and his own exclusion from many areas of decision-making, exist apart from the system in which he finds his *raison d'être*.

Footnotes to Chapter 7

1. On the organization and operation of the indoctrination system in the U.S.S.R., see especially Alex Inkeles, *Public Opinion in Soviet Russia* (Cambridge, Massachusetts: Harvard University Press, 1950); Bruno Kalnins, *Der sowjetische Propagandastaat* (Stockholm: Tidens Förlag, 1956); Samuel N. Harper, *Civic Training in Soviet Russia* (Chicago: University of Chicago Press, 1929); Merle Fainsod, *How Russia is Ruled* (Cambridge, Massachusetts: Harvard University Press, 1954), Chapter VII; Boris Meissner, *Russland im Umbruch* (Frankfurt a/M: Verlag für Geschichte und Politik, 1951), pp. 13-19; and Sidney Harcave, *Structure and Functioning of the Lower Party Organizations in the Soviet Union* (Maxwell Air Force Base, Alabama: Human Resources Research Institute, Technical Research Report Number 23, January, 1954), pp. 4-5, 31, 34-38.

2. From 1934 until 1938 this section, at the Republic level, was called the Section for Culture and Propaganda of Leninism; from 1938 until late 1948 it was called the Propaganda and Agitation Administration.

3. The title of the second highest post in the propaganda section appears to have varied.

4. For a rather different career pattern of a propaganda secretary, see the account of Sosnovskii in Chapter 3·.

5. For the distinction in Soviet usage between "agitation" and "propaganda," see Inkeles, pp. 40-41.

6. Cf. *Stalinskoe Plemia*, August 14, 1940; *RU*, January 29, 1948.

7. *PU*, September 7, 1945. Soviet writers do, however, stress the importance of radio as a propaganda medium; see L. Slepov, *Mestnye partiinye organy: Lektsii prochitannye v Vyshei Partiinoi Shkole pri TsK KPSS, Kafedra Partiinogo Stroitel'stva* [Local Party Organs: Lectures Delivered in the Higher Party School of the Central Committee of the CPSU, Department of Party Structure] (Moscow: Vyshaia Partiinaia Shkola pri TsK KPSS, 1954), p. 49.

8. For a time motion picture production was carried on by a Ministry of Cinematography headed by the former secretary of propaganda of L'vov obkom, Ivan Il'ich Mazepa; more recently, apparently, pictures have been produced by the Ministry of Culture.

9. Before the war called *Komunist*; since then, *Radians'ka Ukraïna* [Soviet Ukraine].

10. See a letter from P. Fishbein and G. Zlenko, journalists in Korsun' raion, criticizing these new recruits; *PU*, July 7, 1956. Cf. Kalnins, p. 197.

11. Aleksandr T. Chekaniuk, Deputy Director of the Propaganda and Agitation Administration of the Central Committee Secretariat, in *PU*, May 5, 1946. 150 persons had been graduated from journalism courses in 1945, including apparently a few trained at a Central Committee course in Kiev. See S. Kachikov, a student in the second course of the Kharkov Party School, "Chto meshaet podgotovke kadrov zhurnalistov" [What Is Interfering With the Preparation of Cadres of Journalists?], *PU*, December 14, 1951.

12. See Chekaniuk's article cited in the preceding footnote.

13. On defects in university training of journalists, see a letter from the deputy editor and the agricultural section director of the Korsun' raion paper in *PU*, July 11, 1956.

14. See the article by S. Kachikov in *PU*, December 14, 1951, cited above.

104 The Soviet Bureaucratic Elite

15. See John A. Armstrong, *Ukrainian Nationalism, 1939-1945* (New York: Columbia University Press, 1955), pp. 229, 239.

16. In the case of the L'vov literary magazine, successive propaganda secretaries were members of the editorial board.

17. *PU*, October 5, 1946.

18. *PU*, September 26, 1946.

19. See Chapter 3.

20. Vladimir Iakovlevich Klimushev, secretary for propaganda of the Stalino obkom, "Ucheba propagandistskikh kadrov v Stalinskoi oblast" [Training of Propagandist Cadres in Stalino Oblast], *PU*, April 25, 1946.

21. *Ibid.*

22. S. Gruzin, director of Nikolaev obkom propaganda and agitation section, "Teoretychna pidhotovka shtatnykh propagandystiv" [Theoretical Preparation of Staff Propagandists], *RU*, April 8, 1950.

23. *PU*, February 23, 1945; *RU*, June 28, 1946, and July 10, 1956.

24. Boris Galin, *Donbas Sketches* (Moscow: Foreign Languages Publishing House, 1948), pp. 135-138. Cf. Kalnins, p. 41, on the influence of higher propaganda officials upon those at the raion or other lower level as compared to the influence of the raikom "line" officials.

25. Speech to the Seventeenth [Ukrainian] Party Congress, *PU*, September 28, 1952.

26. Slepov, p. 15.

27. "Nam potribna ne hazeta, a upovnovazhni" [We Don't Need a Paper, But Plenipotentiaries], *RU*, January 1, 1950. For additional instances in which the higher-level newspapers ardently defended lower-level papers in their criticism of line officials, see *Pravda*, October 25, 1940; *PU*, December 3, 1952; *PU*, February 15, 1951.

28. "Raikom partiï i ioho hazeta" [The Raikom of the Party and Its Newspaper], *RU*, March 16, 1947. For other instances of diversion of journalists to economic work, see *RU*, January 1, 1950 (cited above), and Galin, p. 142.

29. *PU*, December 21, 1955.

30. *PU*, March 3, 1946.

31. *RU*, May 10, 1946.

32. *PU*, February 3, 1949.

33. *RU*, January 29, 1948. Another prewar Komsomol editor, Grigori Trokhimovich Shuiski, became assistant to an (unidentified) Secretary of the Central Committee. *RU*, January 30, 1948.

34. *RU*, June 29, 1950; *PU*, November 25, 1951.

8

The Apparatus in Crisis: Expansion

IN THE SOVIET SYSTEM, as in other systems, numerous features which are obscure under ordinary circumstances are revealed when unusual strains arise. In many respects the Soviet system has operated in a constant state of crisis. It is possible, however, to distinguish periods during which the apparatus as a whole, or its regional branches, has undergone crises of special severity.

The extension of Soviet rule to the West Ukraine provides a peculiar opportunity to observe the adaptation of the Ukrainian apparatus to a situation of unusual difficulty. From the purely physical standpoint the increase in the responsibilities of the apparatus was striking: the nine million inhabitants of the areas annexed between 1939 and 1945 increased the population of the Ukrainian U.S.S.R. by nearly one-third, while the increase in area (about 110,-000 square kilometers) was about twenty-three per cent.

The physical increase was only a minor aspect of the problem confronting the regime, however. Since the new territories had never been under Soviet rule, the long process of elimination of opposition elements and of indoctrination of a new generation had not even begun. Moreover, ideological factors made it very difficult to secure the acceptance of Communism in the West Ukraine. Half of the population consisted of Greek Catholics adhering to Rome though using a Slavonic rite. The Church served as a rallying point for anti-Communist sentiment. In addition, the long struggle of the West Ukrainians against foreign domination had developed a strong nationalist feeling centering around tightly organized conspiratorial parties which carried on a bitter struggle against the new rulers.

Economic and social conditions also made the Communists' task difficult. Even compared to the East Ukraine, rural elements predominated. The Jews, who formed a very large part of the urban population, influenced by their greater fear of the Nazis, had mixed feelings about Communist rule; in any case, they were largely exterminated by the invading Nazis before Communist rule had been firmly established. The Poles, who comprised the former ruling group in most of the annexed territories, were frequently strongly nationalist; they were rarely sympathetic to the Communist regime. Consequently, the urban base of Party activity, which was so important in establishing Communist rule in the East Ukraine, was largely lacking in the West.

Finally, of course, the war itself disrupted Communist control before it could be firmly established. Since the German occupation lasted a year longer in the West Ukraine than in most of the East Ukraine, this disruption was especially serious.

The Soviet Union annexed far the larger part of the western territories during the period of the Nazi-Soviet pact preceding the German invasion of the U.S.S.R. The circumstances of annexation did not differ greatly from area to area; the process of establishment of Soviet rule was correspondingly similar. It is true that the U.S.S.R., taking advantage of the German defeat of Poland, used force to seize the eastern two-fifths of that country. Nevertheless, though the Soviet press at the time devoted much attention to the "glorious" exploits of the Red Army and the NKVD troops, the seizure was practically a military promenade. Similarly, the Red Army was used to occupy Bukovina and Bessarabia, though the Rumanians did not resist.

The Red Army carried out the first phase of Soviet administration as well as the physical occupation. In the former Polish areas the organizing force consisted of the Political Administration of the Ukrainian Front, and the political section of the armed forces also seems to have been in charge in the areas acquired from Rumania.[1] The political officers formed "provisional administrations" in the cities and "peasant committees" in the villages. These bodies, backed by "workers' guards," were nominally responsible for carrying out the initial measures of the new regime, including confiscation and temporary distribution among the poor peasantry of all landed property of the Church and of large private owners.[2]

Even in its first phase, however, the occupation did not assume a strictly military character. The organization of the provisional administrations paralleled that of the usual Soviet administrative system.[3] Moreover, the Ukrainian apparatus was closely associated with the occupation from the beginning. Nikita S. Khrushchev himself accompanied the commander of the "Ukrainian Front," Marshal S. K. Timoshenko.[4] Apparently some technical specialists were sent directly by the neighboring Ukrainian oblast administrations, and these kept in touch with their superiors.[5] While the "agitation echelon" of the Political Administration of the Ukrainian Front was in charge of propaganda activities, Ukrainian apparatus influences were strong. As part of the campaign to picture Soviet rule as a national liberation, the occupation authorities stressed the Ukrainian language. For example, *Vil'na Pratsia* (Free Work), the paper issued by the army authorities in the Polish area, was in Ukrainian. Copies of East Ukrainian papers, such as the Zhitomir *Chervone Polissia* (Red Polessia) and the Republic Ukrainian-language *Komunist* and *Visti*, were sent into the occupied areas.[6] A number of important apparatus officials accompanied these printed representatives of the Ukrainian apparatus. A. T. Chekaniuk, the editor of *Komunist*, supervised the Communization of the L'vov press. The directors of the provisional administrations in a number of cities acquired from Poland and Rumania, apparently including the major centers of L'vov, Kishinev, and Rovno, were Ukrainian apparatus officials.

While the "war situation" officially ended within a few days after the occupation forces arrived, Red Army influence continued for a time, though it progressively diminished as the role of the Ukrainian apparatus increased.[7] Ukrainian Party influences were predominant in the propaganda campaign which accompanied the convocation of a "Ukrainian National Congress" in the former Polish areas at the end of October, 1939, but the Army Political Administration still played an important role.[8]

The Soviet authorities used the National Congress to provide a semblance of popular support for official Soviet annexation of the occupied region. The period of complete ascendancy of the Ukrainian apparatus began on November 15, 1939, with the official incorporation of the territory into the Ukrainian S.S.R. It was not until three weeks later that the Republic Supreme Soviet, by confirming executive committees for six new oblasts, officially extended the Ukrainian administrative system to the new acquisition. At the same time, the Central Committee of the KP(b)U confirmed obkom bureaus for the new provinces.[9] The obkoms did not confirm the raikom bureaus until January, 1940.[10] Apparently the experience gained in the former Polish areas enabled the apparatus to move more swiftly the following year in the territory acquired from Rumania. Within about six weeks after the initial entry of Soviet forces, Soviet authorities announced the formation of two new oblasts in the parts of the occupied territory annexed to the Ukraine.[11]

Absorption of Transcarpathia, the last area acquired in the west, followed a rather different pattern. Officially the U.S.S.R. recognized the sovereignty of Czechoslovakia in this area; apparently, however, Eduard Benes, the Czechoslovak President, had indicated his willingness eventually to cede it to the Soviet Union. Nevertheless, the Soviet regime sought to make sure of the acquisition by presenting the Czechoslovak authorities with a *fait accompli*.[12] Soon after its arrival the Soviet Army admitted official Czechoslovak representatives to part of the area. The Soviet officials, however—especially Lev Mekhlis, the Member of the Military Council (i. e., political officer) of the Fourth Ukrainian Front—restricted Czech official activity.[13] On the other hand, the Army authorities gave a free rein to the activities of Ivan Ivanovich Turianitsia, nominally a political advisor of the Czechoslovak delegation.[14]

Turianitsia, though a native of Transcarpathia, was a veteran Communist. He had been a "Red Guard" in the Hungarian Communist regime of Bela Kun in 1919, when Hungary still held much of Transcarpathia. After Czechoslovakia acquired the territory, he was for a time active in the Czechoslovak Communist Party. From 1930 until 1933, Turianitsia studied in the Kharkov Institute of Journalism. He spent the next six years in Czechoslovakia, but, after the country was absorbed by the Nazis in 1939, he returned to the U.S.S.R., where he apparently remained until his departure with the official delegation for Transcarpathia.[15]

Shortly before the arrival of the Soviet Army, clandestine "People's Committees," with strong Communist participation, sprang up in many localities in Transcarpathia.[16] After the Soviet occupation, these committees were "confirmed" by "popular elections" and new ones were established in the remaining districts. Turianitsia was active in their organization and "packed" them with Communists and other pro-Soviet elements; but at first (October, 1944) he proclaimed that Transcarpathia would remain part of Czechoslovakia.[17] On November 26, 1944, with at least the tacit approval of the Soviet Army authorities, a congress of delegates from the "People's Committees" elected Turianitsia chairman. In spite of his nominal status as an official of the Czechoslovak Republic, he denounced this state at the Mukachevo congress:

> Heavy and joyless has been the life of our people. In the time of the Austro-Hungarian monarchy the Germans and the Hungarians bowed us to the earth. We did not become free in the Czechoslovak Republic, to which we were united without our being consulted, either. The very name of "Czechoslovak Republic" indicates the Carpatho-Ukrainian people was not a member with equal rights. We lived in Czechoslovakia as do orphans in the house of a stepmother.[18]

The congress unanimously adopted a manifesto requesting union with the U.S.S.R. The formal transfer of sovereignty did not take place until November, 1945, primarily because the Czechoslovak authorities secured permission to delay this step until the war had ended in order to avoid constitutional difficulties and a possible precedent for other claims for territorial revision.[19] In early 1946 Transcarpathia became an oblast of the Ukrainian S.S.R., with Turianitsia acting both as chairman of the oblast executive committee and as first secretary of the Party obkom. This unusual arrangement represented a continuation of his dual role as chairman of the National Council and as first secretary of the Communist Party of Transcarpathia, a post he had received soon after the issuance of the manifesto calling for independence.[20]

Others who had collaborated with Turianitsia in the establishment of rule later acquired prominent posts in the Soviet Transcarpathian administration. One of the National Council members, Dmitri M. Tarakovich, became an obkom secretary in 1949, while another, Ivan M. Vash, became first secretary in 1952. Ivan Dmitreevich Petruschhak, a native Transcarpathian who had been a member of the Czechoslovak émigré State Council in London before joining the Czech delegation to Transcarpathia in 1944, was left as the Czech representative when the delegation was forced out at the end of that year. The delegation chief, Nemec, wrote at the time that Petrushchak was "unreliable."[21] He cooperated closely with the Communists and, since the establishment of Soviet rule, he has acted continuously as chairman of the oblast trade union council. It is significant, however, that few, if any, underground or partisan leaders in Transcarpathia attained major posts after the war.[22] Presumably, the rather irregular conditions under which even Communist partisan commanders operated in this remote region made them less reliable than men like Turianitsia, who had been carefully indoctrinated in the U.S.S.R.

In Turianitsia, the Ukrainian Communist Party had ready at hand a thoroughly trained Communist leader of local origin to assume direction of the apparatus in the newly-annexed area. Even in Transcarpathia, however, the second secretary, Grigori Pavlovich Pinchuk, was a member of the East Ukrainian apparatus, having been Director of the School Section of the Central Committee Secretariat.

TABLE 14

NATIONALITY OF OFFICIALS IN DROGOBYCH OBLAST*
(Percentages)

Date	Type of Official	Ukrainian	Russian	Other
1947	Party	71	25	4
	State	77.9	18.1	4.4
1949	Party	84	16	—
	State	100	—	—

* M. D. Men'shov, "Bor'ba kommunisticheskoi partii za sozdanie i vospitanie partiinykh i sovetskikh kadrov v zapadnykh oblastiakh Ukrainskoi S.S.R. v chetvertoi piatiletke (1946-1950 gg.)" [The Struggle of the Communist Party for Creating and Training Party and Soviet Cadres in the Western Oblasts of the Ukrainian S.S.R. in the Fourth Five-Year Plan (1946-1950)], an unpublished dissertation for obtaining the academic degree of candidate of historical sciences in the Institute for Improving the Qualifications of Teachers of Marxism-Leninism, Kiev State University, 1954, p. 62.

In the territories annexed before the war, there was a vast influx of officials from the older parts of the U.S.S.R.

The data from Soviet sources presented in Table 14 indicate that even after the war a considerable proportion of the influx of personnel from the east was Russian. No direct evidence is available on the proportion of Russians sent to western oblasts other than Drogobych, but the fact that Russian-language secondary schools were established in L'vov and Chernovitsy suggests that many newcomers there were Russian, or that at least they desired to have their children educated in the "All-Union" language.

While many of the incoming officials were of Russian nationality, available evidence indicates that most were sent directly from the East Ukrainian apparatus rather than from the R.S.F.S.R. In June, 1940, I. G. Lysenko, Director of the Propaganda Section, implicitly admitted that his branch of the apparatus had drawn heavily on its East Ukrainian personnel to carry on propaganda in the West:

> On the initiative of party organizations of Kiev, Kharkov, Stalino, Voroshilovgrad, Odessa, and Dnepropetrovsk, the best agitators were sent to L'vov, Drogobych, Rovno, Lutsk, Stanislav, and Tarnopol' to give their experience to the local comrades. Altogether, thirty agitators went to the western oblasts of the Ukrainian S.S.R. . . . The Kiev paper *Proletars'ka Pravda*, the papers *Sotsialisticheskii Donbass* [Stalino], *Sotsialistychna Kharkhivshchyna*, *Voroshilovgradskaia Pravda*, *Chernomors'ka Kommuna* [Odessa], *Zoria* [Dnepropetrovsk], and *Dneprovskaia Pravda* [Dnepropetrovsk] sent their best workers to the papers of the western oblasts to give their experience in explaining questions of the electoral campaign.[23]

A recent Soviet student of this question has made an even clearer statement of the role of the East Ukraine in establishing the apparatus in the western areas:

> Only the Communist Party of the Soviet Union, which has many years of experience in the struggle for socialism, could have fulfilled this gigantic task. The Central Committee of the Communist Party of the Ukraine, taking into account the extreme need of the new Soviet territories for experienced cadres

from the first days of the liberation of the West Ukraine, selected and dispatched to the help of the liberated population a significant quantity of Party, Soviet, economic, and other Communist workers from the eastern oblasts of the Republic.

These included 942 Communists sent to Stanislav oblast in December, 1939, alone, and 760 to L'vov in the same period.[24]

These new arrivals included the most important officials. Four of the six obkom first secretaries for the former Polish territories can be identified as having held posts in the East Ukrainian Party bureaucracy; three of the oblast executive committee chairmen had worked in the eastern state bureaucracy. In several of these cases the officials arrived in the western areas just after Soviet invasion, well before the creation of their new positions. In the interval there was apparently an effort to identify these officials with the West Ukraine by having them appear as delegates to the Ukrainian National Congress; the Soviet press covered their elections prominently, but it sedulously avoided all reference to their former positions in the East Ukrainian apparatus.

TABLE 15

BACKGROUNDS OF FIRST SECRETARIES IN THE
WESTERN OBLASTS, 1939-1956*

	Total	L'vov	Stanislav	Drogobych	Ternopol'	Rovno	Volhynia	Chernovitsy	Izmail	Transcarpathia
Total No.	42	6	3	5	4	4	4	6	7	3
No. with previous career in East Ukraine	21	3	1	3	2	2	2	1	6	1
No. with previous career in West Ukraine	15	3	2	2	2	—	1	4	—	1

* The second and third rows of figures are not, of course, mutually exclusive, since it is possible for an official to have had previous careers in both parts of the Ukraine; nor are the columns mutually exclusive, since the same person was in many instances first secretary successively in several oblasts.

The cases just mentioned represent the minimum number of chiefs of the oblast Party and state bureaucracies who came from the East Ukraine, for it is impossible to trace the earlier careers of many of those named to such posts. The figures presented on line 2 of Table 15, which, of course, also represent a minimum, show the continued importance of East Ukrainian apparatus officials in the western obkoms.

At least half of the new assignments as first secretaries went to men who had served in the apparatus of the eastern regions of the Ukraine. In addition to the transfer of East Ukrainians, as the third line of Table 15 indicates, obkom first secretaries often transferred within the West Ukrainian area itself. This tendency was most marked at the formation of the Chernovitsy oblast in August, 1940. At least three of its key officials came from branches of the apparatus established in the former Polish areas just nine months earlier. They included the obkom first secretary, Ivan Samoilovich Grushetskii, who had been second secretary of Stanislav obkom; A. L. Kolikov, the chairman of the oblast executive committee, who had been a deputy chairman in Drogobych oblast; and the obkom third secretary, V. T. Ocheretianyi, who had directed the provisional administration in a city in Ternopol' oblast.

The frequent interchange of personnel among the West Ukrainian oblasts corresponds to a certain unity in the administration of these territories. In this western region of the Ukraine, L'vov acts as a local capital. At the start of the Soviet expansion in Poland, the L'vov provisional administration took precedence by "suggesting" to the administrations of Stanislav, Ternopol', and Lutsk that the National Congress be held.[25] After the Soviet system was more firmly established, the L'vov press, and particularly its periodical publications, served the entire West Ukraine. On at least one occasion L'vov was the scene of a regional meeting of Party officials.[26] It is worth noting, however, that in the transfers and operation of regional "sub-apparatus," the Izmail oblast officials were absent. This is scarcely surprising in view of the fact that this extreme southern part of the territory, acquired from Rumania, is geographically isolated from the other parts of the West Ukraine and has few historical cultural connections with them. Indeed, in

1954 after a long period of separate existence—probably designed to enable the "ironing out" of economic and social differences—Izmail was incorporated in the neighboring Odessa oblast.[27]

Very probably the West Ukraine was treated as a regional unit of the apparatus because the area as a whole had many problems in common. The extreme difficulty of these problems made it a proving ground of special severity for members of the apparatus elite. The initial assignment of heads of the Party and state bureaucracies to the new oblasts seems to have been an occasion for the promotion of promising officials who held important, but not major, posts in the apparatus. The war, which ensued before these men had had the usual "probation period" of two or three years in their new positions, was an especially severe test because of the rapidity of the German advance. Four of the seven obkom first secretaries (excluding Izmail obkom) have not been reported since the outbreak of the war. Possibly they were killed in the fighting; it may be more likely, however, that they were disgraced or that they suffered a still harsher fate for what their superiors felt was failure to live up to their responsibilities in the crisis. A contemporary, anti-Soviet source alleges that L. S. Grishchuk, first secretary of L'vov obkom, was shot, on Khrushchev's orders, for failing to maintain the defenses of the city.[28] On the other hand, those who successfully passed this extreme test seem to be marked for long and successful careers in the apparatus. The three obkom first secretaries who survived have had prominent positions in the apparatus of the Ukraine or other parts of the U.S.S.R. down to 1956.

The oblast executive committee chairmen, only one of whom has disappeared since the outbreak of war, seem to have fared better, possibly because as directors of the routine state administration the regime expected less of them in a crisis. In the vexing, though less dramatic, economic and social tasks confronting the apparatus, however, the state administrators, as well as the Party chiefs, seem to have been on trial.

Probably the most difficult of these tasks was the collectivization of agriculture. As was pointed out in Chapter 5, a major source of the difficulties which the apparatus experienced in dealing with agriculture in the Ukraine has been the small number of politically-trained and reliable personnel in the rural regions. The problem has been far more severe in the West Ukraine than in the country in general. The process of collectivization (practically complete in the East before the emergence of the present elite) requires closer political supervision and consequently more personnel than does the ordinary direction of the kolkhoz system. At the same time, the recent establishment of Soviet rule has meant that there are even fewer Communists in the West Ukrainian countryside than in the East Ukraine. A report on the backgrounds of deputies elected to the soviets (legislative assemblies) of the former Polish areas in December, 1940, indicates how thin Party coverage of the rural areas was at that time. While, in the oblast, raion, and city soviets, one-third to three-fifths of the members belonged to the Party (about 5,000 persons), less than two per cent of the numerous membership of the village soviets were Communists (about 1,500 persons).[29] As late as 1949 the Soviet press praised one West Ukrainian raion because twenty-four of its 107 Party members worked directly in the kolkhozes—though these farms must have contained several thousand peasants.[30]

The gigantic tasks confronting the apparatus in the newly acquired areas and the thin coverage possible with available personnel pointed to the need for rapid recruitment of new personnel from among the local inhabitants. Filling a substantial portion of the apparatus with local people would have other advantages. Presumably they would be better acquainted with conditions in their own areas; they would know the sources of dissatisfaction with the regime and would be better prepared to eliminate the causes or to find and to wipe out the fomentors. The mere presence of local people in the apparatus would tend to demonstrate that the Soviet regime was not a wholly foreign imposition and would thus lessen one cause of dissatisfaction.

At the very beginning of the occupation, considerable numbers of local inhabitants obtained nominally important posts in the provisional administrations. Most of these seem to have been "figure-heads," such as the peasants and workers customarily elected to the Supreme Soviet, Congress delegations, and other assemblies. A few,

on the other hand, were Communists who emerged from the underground when the Red Army appeared.

Communists of the illegal Party organizations in Poland were,
indeed, a natural source of local recruits for the apparatus. The
ambiguous position of these organizations complicated matters,
however. Until 1938, the Polish Communist Party was a regular
section of the Communist International. At that time the Comintern
took the almost unprecedented step of ordering the Polish Party to
disband. In February, 1956, the Soviet press "posthumously"
exonerated the Polish Communist Party; apparently its dissolution
had been the result of Stalin's frenzy against suspected opponents
everywhere.

Soviet sources published after the annexation of Eastern Poland—
but during Stalin's lifetime—ignore the existence of the Polish
Communist Party and refer only to the "Communist Party of the
West Ukraine," which had been an autonomous section of the
Polish Party. There were undoubtedly a number of relatively obscure Party members in the West Ukrainian areas occupied by the
Red Army in the autumn of 1939. Several of these—apparently
those who had been in prison for several years and who had thus
not been involved in the "deviation" of the Party—were hailed as
martyrs and elected to the National Congress.[31] There is even a
report of an instance in which the Red Army authorities turned to
one of these liberated Communists for advice on the appointment
of a local man to a prominent post in a raion provisional administration.[32]

After a brief period of prominence the former underground
Communists appear to have sunk back into obscurity. Several became students, preparing for comparatively unimportant careers
(from the political standpoint), such as that of agricultural specialist.[33] Quite possibly this de-emphasis of the local Communists was
part of a general policy of harsher treatment of the inhabitants of
the West Ukraine which the regime apparently instituted after the
first few months of occupation had shown that the population was
not inclined to be grateful for the establishment of Soviet rule.[34]

The German conquest of the West Ukraine in the early summer of
1941 seems to have increased the prestige of the local Communists.

Probably the failure of many of the "imported" apparatus officials made the local men, by contrast, appear more reliable. Their knowledge of local conditions and of experience in "conspiratorial" conditions of the Party under Polish rule fitted them for underground work against the Germans. For example, Terenti Fedorovich Novak, who had been a member of the underground regional committee of the Polish province of Volhynia, was assigned to head an underground group working against the Germans in that area. Before Novak left, his superior, V. A. Begma, the Rovno obkom secretary, told him:

> The party knows you as an old underground worker and a good organizer. We believe in your strength, Comrade Novak, in your steadfastness, in your faculty for self-sacrifice. But the Party is sending you not to a heroic death, but to responsible Party work. The strictest conspiratorial conditions are necessary—you do not need to be instructed in this.[35]

After the war most of the underground Communists again disappeared from public notice, but a few have continued to occupy prominent, though secondary, positions in the apparatus. One of the most interesting is Mariia Semenovna Kikh. Although born of a peasant family in the L'vov area, she had been a member of the Party since 1932. She was arrested for Communist activity in 1936 and remained in a Polish prison until the arrival of the Red Army. Soon afterwards she played a prominent part in the Ukrainian National Congress as "a representative of youth." In 1940 she was a student at L'vov University, without, however, giving up political work. During the war she became, after training in Moscow, a radio operator for a partisan group in the West Ukraine. Immediately after the close of hostilities she was prominent in propaganda work in L'vov, and a few years later she became a staff member of the oblast Party school. Not long afterwards she was elected to the high honorary post of Deputy Chairman of the Presidium of the Supreme Soviet of the Ukraine, and in 1955 she received the relatively important apparatus assignment of deputy chairman of the L'vov oblast executive committee. Somewhere, in the course of this promising career, she found time to become a mother.

Reliable underground Communists like Mariia Kikh, capable of absorbing training for important posts in the apparatus, were far too few to satisfy the Party's need for local recruits for the apparatus. Consequently, especially in the immediate postwar period, the Party emphasized the "development" of cadres from among the general population.

> Only political blindness, only a narrow outlook, a failure to understand what the Party demands at the present stage, explains the lack of desire on the part of some directors to notice the people growing up around them. What, for example, is one to think of the effort of the secretary of the Ratno raikom of the KP(b)U in Volhynia, Comrade Goriun, to present the isolation of the raikom from local activists as "the natural order of things"? The secretaries of the Ivanichi and Olyka raikoms of the KP(b)U, Comrades Kaspruk and Seliutin, regret the lack of cadres and wait for one to send them cadres who are already qualified, but do not want to develop the local people. And even in Lutsk itself—under the nose of the Volhynian obkom of the KP(b)U—the Lutsk raikom of the KP(b)U to this very day has not really worked with the local cadres, has not drawn people from among the local activists.[36]

While the Party needed locally-recruited personnel especially in predominantly rural areas like Volhynia, Party authorities also wanted officials of local origin in urban centers like L'vov. Here part of the pressure for enlisting the aid of local "activists" apparently originated with local Communists who had already attained some influence in the apparatus.[37] As in Volhynia, however, it took considerable pressure from higher authorities to induce the predominantly East Ukrainian apparatus officials to move in this direction.

> But, in the meantime, there is a large reserve in the city for assignment to directing work. In the gorkom they love to show off figures on the hundreds of local Ukrainian workers who have now become shop superintendents and foremen of mills and factories, chairmen of artels [collectives], directors of stores, etc. But the gorkom and the raikom poorly utilize these people, rarely meet and consult with them, take little trouble about their development. And if you present them with the question, "Who

of these can be assigned further to directing work?" the secretary for cadres of the gorkom, Comrade Klimov, and the instructors will have difficulty in presenting a few names.[38]

The Soviet regime placed special emphasis on securing new administrative personnel from among the lower strata of pre-Soviet
society. A highly publicized case immediately after the Red Army
invasion concerned one Hertsog, a young worker in the L'vov streetcar system. Through listening to the Moscow radio every midnight—
so the story went—he had learned "stakhanovite" (shock-worker)
methods. Putting them into practice when the Polish administration
disappeared, he started the streetcar lines operating again, then
placed the functioning system at the disposal of the Army administration.[39]

Such an account was useful as an example of "proletarian" ability.
The Party was well aware, however, that Lenin's 1917 theory that
the average workman could undertake the most complicated administrative tasks had proved impracticable. Even official propaganda concerning the use of personnel from the lower classes frequently stressed the long process of training under Party aegis. The
story of Ul'iana Vasilivna Efimchuk-Diachuk, an illiterate hired
farm laborer before the Soviet occupation who eventually rose to the
post of deputy chairman of the Rovno oblast executive committee,
was a typical occasion for self-congratulation by Party officials:
"The Party knew how to discover the gifted woman from among a
hundred thousand villagers."[40]

However attractive from the standpoint of Communist theory,
the selection and training of uneducated peasants and workers was a
difficult method of filling the ranks of the apparatus. At first sight
the considerable West Ukrainian intellectual and professional class
would seem much more promising material. Apparently the Party
also took this view, for considerable effort was devoted to securing
the support of this group immediately after the arrival of the Soviet
forces. It is true that a considerable number of the intellectuals who
had been active in non-Communist political groups were arrested,
or that they escaped by flight to German-occupied territory. Many
professional men found it necessary or advisable to take obscure
jobs in other lines of work. Still, a physician, M. I. Panchishin, was

elected chairman of the National Congress; this body and the provisional administration contained many other physicians, professors,
and engineers. In the incorporation of Transcarpathia the Soviet
authorities emphasized still more strongly the enlistment of col-
laborators from among the educated group. Even priests, an important element in the West Ukrainian intellectual stratum, were
included, though the Soviet press had bitterly denounced their
efforts five years earlier to "infiltrate" the National Congress in the
former Polish areas.[41]

Apparently the long-range effect of these efforts to enlist the West
Ukrainian "intelligentsia" was slight. The Party itself recognized
the difficulty of indoctrinating persons who had been educated in a
non-Communist environment, especially when they had become
imbued with Ukrainian nationalism, as had a great many West
Ukrainian intellectuals.[42] One of the highest positions attained by a
West Ukrainian intellectual who was not a Party member before the
establishment of Soviet rule went to a Galician journalist of peasant
stock, Kuz'ma Nikolaevich Pelekhatyi. As a youth before World
War I, when the area was part of the Austro-Hungarian Empire, he
was imprisoned for radical activities. Between the wars he worked as
a journalist and was again imprisoned for "revolutionary demo-
cratic" activity by the Poles. He welcomed the establishment of the
Soviet regime and continued his profession as a staff member of the
L'vov oblast newspaper. During World War II he edited underground propaganda leaflets, and in 1946 he was elected deputy
chairman of the L'vov city executive committee. It was not until
1948 that he entered the Communist Party, however; the following
year he was promoted to the relatively high position of chairman of
the L'vov oblast executive committee.[43]

That Pelekhatyi was an exception is indicated by the admission
by a Soviet source that, in 1946, there were only two other major
officials of local origin in the L'vov city administration: the procurator and another deputy chairman.[44] Significantly, all three
were officials of the state bureaucracy rather than of the more
powerful Party machine. At that time a considerable portion of the
lower personnel was already of local origin, as shown in Table 16,

but only a few of those in higher capacities were natives of the West Ukraine.

TABLE 16

PROPORTION OF WEST UKRAINIAN OFFICIALS OF
LOCAL ORIGIN, 1946*

Oblast	% Local in Nomenklatura of Obkom	% Local in Nomenklatura of Gorkoms and Raikoms
Stanislav	23	73
Volhynia	14.8	65
Drogobych	16.6	59.5
L'vov	11.5	58.3

*Men'shov, p. 43.

In the following years, considerable efforts were made to increase the proportion of West Ukrainians. So many new appointments were made (largely from among graduates of the obkom and Republic Party schools) that by 1949 forty-five per cent of the Party officials and 23.2 per cent of the state officials had served less than one year in their posts.[45]

By 1954 a Soviet source could boast that all of the oblast executive committee chairmen were local men. It is noteworthy, however, that the West Ukrainians continued to occupy a much more prominent place in the state bureaucracy than in the more powerful Party posts (cf. Table 14).

Though there undoubtedly had been some progress between 1946 and 1953 in securing local recruits for the apparatus, the charge of "Russification" and the predominance of East Ukrainians formed a major portion of the indictment of L. G. Mel'nikov on his dismissal from the first secretaryship in June, 1953. This charge was repeated at the plenums of several of the West Ukrainian obkoms and led to the demotion of K. Z. Litvin, a major figure in the propaganda branch. With the downfall of Lavrenti Beria in late June, the attack on the personnel policy subsided. Soviet sources have since maintained that the "Russification" charges were part of a far-reaching plot organized by Beria to gain control of the Ukrainian police apparatus, to form an alliance with "bourgeois nationalists," and eventually to overthrow the Soviet regime. While this story seems fantastic, the regime's sensitivity to attacks on its West Ukrainian personnel policy indicates that the West Ukraine is far from securely incorporated in the Soviet system.[46]

The overall picture of the adaptation of the Ukrainian apparatus to the crisis of expansion in the West is, therefore, a mixed one. Certainly the apparatus elite was able to provide sufficient high officials to staff the most important posts in the new areas. To some extent the expansion even provided a useful testing ground for rising officials. The organizational arrangement, particularly the development of the regional sub-unit of the apparatus, indicates a considerable degree of adaptability to novel circumstances. The continued deficiency of West Ukrainian recruits for the apparatus represents a serious failure, however. While it may in large measure be explained by the inherent difficulty of winning over and of preparing people from this area for responsible positions, very likely it is partly a result of the incapacity of the existing elite to deal with persons not brought up under the Soviet system. It may well be due also to a desire of this elite to maintain its own monopoly of important positions in the Ukrainian apparatus.

Footnotes to Chapter 8

1. On the former Polish areas, see A. Mareev, battalion commissar, "Vremenye upravleniia i krest'ianskie komitety—organy revoliutsionoi narodnoi vlasti" [The Provisional Administrations and the Peasant Committees—Organs of the Revolutionary Popular Power], *Partiino-Politicheskaia Rabota v RKKA*, No. 21 (November), 1939, pp. 45-46. For confirmation by a non-Army source, see *Visti*, September 20, 1939. For the Rumanian areas, the scanty information available indicates that the same situation prevailed; see *Krasnaia Zvezda*, July 12, 1940.

2. *Visti*, September 29, 1939.

3. See *Kolhospnyk Ukraïny*, September 26, 1939, and *Visti*, September 29, 1939.

4. *Visti*, September 20, 1939.

5. A group of communications workers from Zhitomir was sent to the border town of Korets; from there they got in touch by telephone with M. A. Siromiatnikov, the first secretary of the Zhitomir obkom; see *Visti*, September 20, 1939. This same unit was apparently later in Rovno; see *Visti*, September 21, 1939.

6. *Visti*, September 20, 1939, and September 24, 1939.

7. The "war situation" ended in Ternopol' *voevod*, the easternmost section of the areas acquired from Poland, at 5:00 p.m. on September 25, 1939 (*Krasnaia Zvezda*, September 30, 1939).

8. *Visti*, October 9, 1939.

9. *Visti*, December 9, 1939.

10. Grigori Ivanovich Lomov "Ustanovlenie i ukreplenie sovetskoi vlasti v zapadnoi Ukraine (1939-1941 gg.)" [Establishment and Strengthening of Soviet Power in the West Ukraine (1939-1941)], an unpublished dissertation for obtaining the academic degree of candidate of historical sciences in the Institute of History of the Ukraine, Academy of Sciences of the Ukrainian S.S.R., 1953 (L'vov), p. 230.

11. See *Stalinskoe Plemia*, August 21, 1940, for the confirmation of the obkom bureaus.

12. For a detailed discussion of Czechoslovak-Soviet relations concerning Transcarpathia and particularly the events in the area during 1944, see Frantisek Nemec and Vladimir Moudry, *The Soviet Seizure of Subcarpathian Ruthenia* (Toronto: William B. Anderson, 1955). Nemec was the principal Czechoslovak representative in the area. Vasyl Markus, in *L'Incorporation de l'Ukraine Subcarpathique à l'Ukraine Soviétique, 1944-1945* (Louvain: Centre Ukrainien d'Etudes en Belgique, 1956), presents a Ukrainian nationalist account. For an analysis of events in Transcarpathia, I am also much indebted to Capt. Berry, U.S.A., who prepared a paper on this subject for my seminar at the Russian Institute, Columbia University, 1957.

13. See Nemec and Moudry, p. 161, on the ascendancy of Mekhlis over the Red Army military commander.

14. *Ibid.*, p. 85, and the contemporary document reproduced on pp. 271-277. On the other hand, Turianitsia's obituary in the Soviet press states that he went to Transcarpathia as a commissar of the Third Special Brigade of the Czechoslovak Corps which was formed during the war in the U.S.S.R. (*RU*, March 29, 1955).

15. *Ibid.*

16. I. F. Evseev, *Narodnye Komitety Zakarpatskoi Ukrainy: Organy gosudarstvennoi vlasti (1944-1945)* [The People's Committees of Transcarpathian Ukraine: Organs of the State Power (1944-1945)] (Moscow: Gosudarstvennoe Izdatel'stvo Iuridicheskoi Literatury, 1955), pp. 54-57.

17. Nemec and Moudry, pp. 92, 103.

18. *PU*, December 23, 1944.

19. Nemec and Moudry, p. 176.

20. *RU*, March 29, 1955.

21. Nemec and Moudry, p. 339.

22. The secretary of the Transcarpathian section of the Czechoslovak Communist Party, Aleksei Borkaniuk, led the underground movement during 1941-1942 but was arrested and executed by the Hungarian regime (Evseev, p. 50). On the other hand, there is some evidence that persons who had collaborated with the Magyars were given minor posts at the beginning (Nemec and Moudry, p. 103), and it is possibly significant that a Magyar paper was permitted by the Red Army authorities (*Ibid.*, p. 248). This paper is one of the two remaining papers in the Ukrainian S.S.R. published in languages other than Russian and Ukrainian.

23. I. H. Lysenko, "V zapadnykh oblastiakh Ukrainy" [In the Western Oblasts of the Ukraine], *Partiinoe Stroitel'stvo*, No. 4, 1940, p. 24.

24. Lomov, p. 229.

25. "Rik suspil'noi perebudovy politychnoho i ekonomichnoho zhyttia v zakhidnykh oblastiakh U.S.S.R." [A Year of Social Reconstruction of Political and Economic Life in the Western Oblasts of the Ukrainian S.S.R.], *Bil'shovyk Ukrainy*, September, 1940, p. 12.

26. This was a meeting of propaganda directors; *PU*, August 19, 1941.

27. Before the war Izmail oblast was known as Akkerman oblast. The city of Akkerman has been renamed Belgorod-Dnestrovskii.

28. *Krakivs'ki Visti*, August 14, 1941.

29. Based on tables in *Stalinskoe Plemia*, December 19, 1940.

30. *RU*, April 2, 1949.

31. See Ol. Matov, "Khvliuiuchi dokumenty" [Perturbing Documents], *Visti*, October 22, 1939; and Ol. Matov, "Za krashchykh siniv narodu" [For the Best Sons of the People], *Visti*, October 29, 1939.

32. Dmitrii Medvedev, *Sil'nye dukhom* [The Strong in Spirit] (Moscow: Voennoe Izdatel'stvo Voennogo Ministerstva Soiuza S.S.R., 1951), pp. 219-221, 226.

33. *Ibid*, ,p. 221.

34. John A. Armstrong, *Ukrainian Nationalism, 1939-1945* (New York: Columbia University Press, 1955), pp. 68-69.

35. Medvedev, p. 220.

36. "Po-stalinski rastit' mestnye kadry v zapadnykh oblastiakh" [Develop Local Cadres in the Western Oblasts in the Stalinist Fashion], *PU*, September 28, 1946.

37. Mariia Kikh, "Rastet nashe vliianie na molodezh' " [Increase Our Influence On Youth], *PU*, March 18, 1945.

38. "Kak podbiraiut i vospityaiut kadry v L'vove" [How Cadres Are Chosen and Trained in L'vov], *PU*, July 6, 1946.

39. D. Min, *Zapadnaia Ukraina* [The West Ukraine] (Moscow: Gosudars-

tvennoe Izdatel'stvo Politicheskoi Literatury, 1939), p. 48; *Pravda*, September 28, 1939.

40. V. A. Begma, "Mistsevyi aktyv—opora partiinoï orhanizatsii'." [The Local Activist—The Support of the Party Organization], *RU*, November 24, 1948.

41. See M. S. Burmistenko, "Vossoedinenie velikogo ukraniskogo naroda v edinom ukrainskom gosudarstve" [Union of the Great Ukrainian People in a Single Ukrainian State], *Partiinoe Stroitel'stvo*, No. 22, December, 1939, pp. 23-24.

42. See, for example, "Do kintsy vykryty burzhuazno natsionalistychni kontseptsiï Hrushevs'koho i ioho 'shkoly' " [The Final Unmasking of the Bourgeois Nationalist Conceptions of Hrushevskii and His "School"], *RU*, September 14, 1946.

43. Most of this information is based on his obituary in *PU*, March 29, 1952.

44. "Kak podbiraiut i vospityaiut kadry v L'vove" [How Cadres Are Selected and Trained in L'vov], *PU*, July 6, 1946.

45. Men'shov, p. 62.

46. Ivan Andreevich Fateev, "Bor'ba Kommunisticheskoi Partii Sovetskogo Soiuza za povyshenie bditel'nosti sovetskogo naroda v poslevoennyi period (1945-1953 gg.)" [The Struggle of the Communist Party of the Soviet Union for Heightening the Vigilance of the Soviet People During the Postwar Period (1945-1953)], an unpublished dissertation for obtaining the academic degree of candidate of historical sciences in the Department of History of the CPSU, Kiev State University, 1954 (revised 1956).

9

The Apparatus in Crisis: War

Iᶠ THE WESTWARD EXPANSION of the Ukrainian S.S.R. provided a significant test of the ability of the apparatus to meet new demands, the German invasion of 1941 was a far more drastic trial. Within four months after the outbreak of war on June 22, all except the eastern extremity of the Ukraine had been conquered; the last invaders were not to be expelled until September, 1944. Throughout most of the intervening period the apparatus, as a machine directing the affairs of a large nation, necessarily ceased to function. The complex structure of Party and state bureaucracies did not entirely dissolve, however, and the majority of the officials who constituted it continued to play a part in the Soviet system. It is, therefore, possible to speak of the role of the Ukrainian apparatus during the war and, indeed, to learn much concerning its nature from an examination of this period.

The first two months of war were a period of almost unrelieved disaster for the Soviet armies and of near chaos in the administration. During this period the entire area acquired from Poland and Rumania in 1939-1940 was lost, and with it almost all of the East Ukraine west of the Dnieper. Only an isolated coastal enclave at Odessa and a bridgehead, including Kiev, held out.

The maintenance of control over the capital until September 19, 1941, did, however, enable the apparatus to recover a measure of stability. When the retreat began again, however, it was in some respects even more catastrophic than it had been during the summer. Using their favorite maneuver of double envelopment, the German forces surrounded the large forces defending Kiev. A number of important Party leaders concentrated in the Kiev area fled with great difficulty. Several, including the Second Secretary of the Central Committee, M. A. Burmistenko, and the first secretary of the Zhitomir obkom, M. A. Siromiatnikov, apparently perished.[1]

After the capture of the capital the Germans rapidly occupied all of the remainder of the Ukraine, except Voroshilovgrad oblast. Probably a majority of the surviving members of the apparatus received assignments in the general Soviet war effort; as late as 1949, forty-one per cent of the delegates of the Sixteenth Party Congress were persons who had taken a "direct part" in the war.[2] Nikita Khrushchev himself assumed the duty of Member of the Military Council (i.e., chief political officer) of the Southwest Front. He held this post—or the corresponding posts in the Council of the Voronezh Front and the First Ukrainian Front—throughout most of the war. Khrushchev's example in assuming military-political duties was followed by a great many of his subordinates. Zakhar Fedorovich Oleinyk, deputy chairman of the Kiev city soviet, became successively plenipotentiary of the Military Councils of the Southwest, Southeast, Southern, Stalingrad, and Voronezh Fronts; then in June, 1943, he became Member of the Military Council of the thirty-eighth Army of the First Ukrainian Front.[3] Officials in more specialized branches of administration seem to have been assigned as a rule to similar types of work in the Army. The chairman of an oblast court became a member of a military tribunal; the editor of the Sumy oblast paper became editor of a division newspaper.[4]

Men with training and experience in industrial management, on the other hand, appear to have been deliberately kept out of military service.[5] For example, Anatolii Nikolaevich Kuzmin, director of the "Zaprozhstal' " steel combine, became director of a metallurgical plant in Novosibirsk. Semen Borisovich Zadionchenko, the first secretary of the Dnepropetrovsk obkom, assumed the corresponding post in Kemerovo oblast; in his new post, as in Dnepropetrovsk, he supervised some of the major metallurgical centers of the U.S.S.R.[6]

While assignments to posts in the R.S.F.S.R. appear to have gone most frequently to economic specialists, Ivan Alekseivich Sosnovskii, propaganda secretary of Odessa oblast and a career specialist in ideological work, was assigned to the corresponding post in Krasnoiarsk *krai* (territory) in the R.S.F.S.R.[7] As noted previously, a much larger segment of the propaganda group appears to have been engaged in preparing materials to be spread among the Ukrainian population which had been evacuated or to be sent through underground means to those living under enemy occupation.[8]

The aspects of the participation of the apparatus in the war which have received the most publicity in Soviet publications are the underground and partisan movements.[9] By the first week of July the Secretariat of the Central Committee was beginning to put into effect an elaborate plan for operations in the rear of the enemy. The plan had apparently been prepared before the outbreak of war, although at that time only the highest officials knew of it.[10] The scheme called for the creation of a complete network of clandestine Party organizations, paralleling that of the existing Party, to serve as the directing centers for sabotage, spying, and partisan activities. The underground obkom was to direct all such disruptive activities in its oblast and was to have immediate charge of an oblast partisan detachment; each raikom was to have a raion detachment. Numerous factors, including the rapidity of the German advance and the panic it caused in Party circles as well as in the general population, prevented the implementation of this plan. In the newly-acquired western oblasts, apparently, nothing was done before the Germans arrived, although not long after the Soviet evacuation a few trusted Party members were sent back through the lines to form underground centers.[11] In the oblasts west of the Dnieper the Germans encountered a number of scattered partisan detachments along the banks of the Bug and the Dniester.[12] A vigorous underground was formed in Odessa.[13]

Along the Dnieper, where resistance was more prolonged, much more could be done to carry out the plan for a network of underground headquarters; nearly one-half of the Kiev oblast raions contained underground raikoms.[14] The city itself contained, according to Soviet sources, thirty-seven different underground groups; German police reports also note the frequency with which new underground groups were uncovered.[15]

The "investment" of Party personnel in these desperate operations was considerable. Thirty-six hundred Communists, including 500 members of the underground obkom and raikoms, were said to have been dispatched to underground and partisan work in Kiev oblast alone.[16] The initial Stalino oblast underground organization had 525 members.[17] Other early groups consisted almost entirely of Party members and NKVD officials. For example, a German report indicates that a group of 650 partisans near Nikopol' consisted principally of NKVD border troops and security units from the larger cities and evacuated territories, Party officials, and militia units formed from the workers of Krivoi Rog before it was evacuated.[18] Soviet sources also maintain that during this early period Party members and officials predominated in the partisan detachments, although these sources do not reveal the major role of the NKVD.[19]

During this first period the organization of the partisans was supervised by M. A. Burmistenko and, under him, the first secretaries of the obkoms. Less important officials were chosen to carry on the risky tasks of direction of activity behind enemy lines, however. Apparently the highest official assigned to such work at this period was A. F. Fedorov, the first secretary of Chernigov obkom. The Stalino underground obkom, for example, was composed of such relatively minor officials as the former secretary of a rural raikom and two former Party organizers for coal mines.[20]

The rapidity of the German advance, the severe measures which they took in some areas to stamp out the partisan activity, and, above all, the unsuitability of the open steppe of the southern Ukraine led to an almost complete elimination of partisan activity in this area during the autumn of 1941.[21] A few groups survived, however, in the forest and swamp area on the northern border of the Ukraine. Notable among them was the Chernigov underground organization. In the adjacent Sumy oblast the famous Kovpak partisan band had a raion detachment as its original nucleus. A few other detachments, including two composed of workers and officials from Kharkov, joined the remnants of various Russian partisan detachments in the large Briansk forest in Orel oblast (R.S.F.S.R.). The Party-organized partisans in this area were heavily augmented by soldiers of Red Army and of NKVD units cut off in the German encirclements.

After the successful defense of Moscow indicated Soviet ability to carry on a protracted war, great efforts were devoted to the re-

organization and expansion of the partisan movement. T. A. Strokach, before the war Deputy People's Commissar of Internal Affairs
of the Ukraine, became chief of the staff of the Ukrainian Movement, formed on June 20, 1942, though Khrushchev was nominally
in charge.[22] Strokach maintained his headquarters in Moscow
throughout most of the period before the reconquest of the Ukraine.
He was actively assisted in partisan direction by Moisei S. Spivak,
the former Secretary for Cadres, and Iosif Titovich Tabulevich,
who had been director of the Labor Reserves Section of the Central
Committee Secretariat.[23] In early June, 1943, Strokach did, however, make a visit by airplane to partisan-held areas behind the
German lines. D. S. Korotchenko, the third secretary, stayed in the
partisan area from April 19 to July 4, 1943, while a number of less
important officials of the Central Committee Secretariat spent
varying periods of time with the partisans.[24]

In addition to the Party and NKVD officials who had survived
among the partisan leaders in the Ukraine, a number of new leaders
appeared in 1943. The most important Ukrainian official in this
group was V. A. Begma, who returned to his former Party area,
Rovno oblast, in early 1943 to organize partisan activity and to
head the underground obkom.[25] The very fact that he returned
so late, however, is indicative of the limited success of the underground and partisan activities in this area during the early stages
of the war. Even in the easternmost regions of the Ukraine, where
months rather than days had been available for preparation, the
underground almost collapsed during the first winter of the war.
In one raion of Stalino oblast, twenty-seven of the thirty-three
Communists assigned to underground activity fled before the enemy
arrived. The oblast organization, in general, was poorly organized
and it was infested with traitors; some of its agents even went over
to the Germans. Failure was so complete that in May, 1942, the
regular Stalino obkom created a new organization from among
evacuated Party members who were then sent behind the enemy
lines. The confusion of the situation is indicated by the fact that
this was called the "parallel underground obkom."[26]

It seems probable that the Ukrainian apparatus officials were a
minority among the partisan commanders during the period of

extensive partisan activity from late 1942 to early 1944. Alongside them were numerous Party officials from other parts of the U.S.S.R., such as Dmitri Medvedev, the first organizer of the underground movement in the Rovno area, and many regular officers of the Red Army. The rank-and-file partisans, while largely Ukrainian, were chiefly peasants recruited in the rural areas where the partisan bands operated. The remarkable change in composition of the total partisan force is reflected in the small proportion of Party members among the total number of partisans operating in the Ukraine during the war, in spite of the prevalence of Party members at the early stage. Of a total of 220,000 partisans, only 14,875 were Communists —seven per cent, or about the same proportion as that of the Communists in the total Ukrainian male population of military age.[27] Similarly, the 26,000 Komsomols among the partisans represented about the same proportion as that of the Communist youth organization in the general population available for military service.

By the latter stages of the war the partisan movement as a whole had ceased to constitute an elite body drawn from the apparatus. The fact that sixty-six of the delegates to the Sixteenth Party Congress (1949) had led partisan detachments indicates that the movement continued to be a proving ground for development of new elite members, however. More evidence for this assertion is easily obtained by tracing the careers of numerous partisan chieftains after the war. Fedorov and Begma, already obkom first secretaries before the war, have risen no higher. However, two of Fedorov's lieutenants became obkom first secretaries, one became an oblast executive chairman, and two became subordinate secretaries in the Chernigov obkom. Most of these had been well started on their careers in the Chernigov apparatus before the war began.

The most complete information is available on Fedorov's subordinates, but it is apparent that leading partisan officers from other groups also received major posts after the war. For example, Zakhar Antonovich Bogatyr', second in command of the Saburov band, had been chairman of a L'vov oblast raion executive committee in 1941. Shortly after the war he was appointed deputy chairman of the Kiev oblast executive committee and he later became chairman of Zhitomir oblast executive committee. Oddly enough, two of the three members of the original, unsuccessful Stalino obkom were promoted after the war. M. A. Platonov, the raikom secretary, became deputy secretary of the obkom, while S. N. Shchetinin, a Party mine organizer, became secretary of Stalino gorkom.

Several of the liaison officers who assisted Strokach and Korotchenko in controlling the partisan activities later became important officials of the Central Committee Secretariat. Strokach himself has been Minister of the Interior of the Ukraine during most of the post-war period. Among the NKVD officials who became prominent as partisan leaders, Saburov, a petty NKVD official in Kiev before the war, became chief of the MVD administration in the important frontier oblast of Drogobych, while Mikhail Ivanovich Naumov, who had commanded a renowned partisan cavalry detachment, has directed the MVD in Chernovitsy oblast—also a frontier district—for many years.

Part of the prominence accorded these figures is doubtless due to the fact that their wartime records made them suitable figures for public glorification. It is significant that the great majority were already officials of some importance in the apparatus before the war, however. Only a very few "little men"—such as Sidor Artemovich Kovpak, a semi-literate petty official in Putivl' raion before the war—have become prominent solely as a result of their partisan careers. Even Kovpak has held honorific positions, such as that of Vice Chairman of the Presidium of the Supreme Soviet, rather than assignments of real responsibility. The major significance of the partisan episode in the history of the apparatus seems to have been that of a testing ground for those who were already started on Party careers.[28]

While a large portion of the apparatus was engaged in partisan activities or in the general war effort apart from any direct connection with Ukrainian affairs, a skeleton structure of Ukrainian state, Party, and cultural organizations existed in unoccupied parts of the U.S.S.R. After the fall of Kiev some activities were maintained for a short time in Voroshilovgrad, but, although this city was not captured until late summer of 1942, it was apparently too close to the front for safe direction of Party activities. The principal newspaper, *Komunist*, appeared in Starobelsk in the northern part of

Voroshilovgrad oblast, while Khrushchev and some other prominent figures, such as the writer Korneichuk, were in Voronezh with the Red Army headquarters during the height of the German advance in the south in November, 1941.[29]

In their drive on Stalingrad during the summer of 1942 the German forces overran the last unconquered remnants of the Ukrainian S.S.R. The newspaper *Komunist* and some other propaganda installations were withdrawn to Saratov, over three hundred miles from the nearest Ukrainian territory, but a major portion of the apparatus was centered in Moscow: "There were many top men of the Central Committee of the Ukrainian Communist Party and the Ukrainian Government living in the Moskva Hotel at the time."[30] Cultural institutions were withdrawn to areas still more remote. For example, the University of Odessa was evacuated to Maikop in the North Caucasus in late 1941, then in 1942 to Bairam Ali in the Turkmen S.S.R.[31] The Kiev motion picture studio was transferred to Ashkabad, the capital of the Turkmen S.S.R.[32] The principal cultural institutions, including the Academy of Sciences and some state institutions, were evacuated to Ufa, the capital of the Bashkir A.S.S.R. Apparently Komsomol headquarters was also located there.[33] Factories were relocated in a number of eastern industrial centers, especially those in the southern Urals and the Kuznets Basin.[34]

After the encirclement of the German Sixth Army at Stalingrad, the Red Army pushed rapidly westward, and by the end of December, 1942, it had regained a foothold on Ukrainian territory in the northern part of Voroshilovgrad oblast.[35] The actions of the Party in this period suggest that it believed the Soviet recovery to be permanent and that it was determined to press its psychological advantage by reestablishing the apparatus on Ukrainian soil as soon as possible. In early 1943 some Party and state offices, including the Propaganda and Agitation Section, were set up in Kabychivka, a village near Voroshilovgrad which was jokingly referred to as the "capital." *Komunist* began publication in Markovka, in the extreme northeastern part of Voroshilovgrad oblast.[36] On February 16, 1943, the Soviet forces reoccupied Kharkov. Within a few days after the Germans were forced out, Aleksei Alekseevich Epishev, the obkom first secretary, set up an improvised headquarters and began reorganizing the administrative structure.[37] On March 15, however, the Germans recaptured Kharkov, and until late summer the Ukrainian front remained fairly stable. Then began a series of sweeping Soviet victories; during August and September, 1943, practically all of the area east of the Dnieper was reconquered. During this period the Soviet press devoted considerable attention to the restoration of the Party and state apparatus in the areas regained. At the end of August, Viktor Mikhailovich Churaev, who had replaced Epishev as obkom first secretary, opened a triumphal gathering in Kharkov which was attended by Khrushchev, Korotchenko, and other leading Party personalities.[38] Stalino was not recaptured until September 7, but the following day workers of the gorkom, the obkom, the oblast executive committee, and the coal combine were already back in the city.[39] Mikhail Ivanovich Drozhzhin, the obkom first secretary, and Filipp Nestorovich Reshetniak, the oblast executive committee chairman, had returned by the middle of the month.[40]

The Soviet press placed less emphasis on the resumption of Party activities west of the Dnieper during late 1943 and 1944, perhaps because the victorious advance was by then a familiar story. Occasional items indicate, however, that the apparatus was reinstalled in those areas as quickly as in the eastern regions.[41] Moreover, there was surprisingly little turnover in the major officials of the apparatus, considering the enormous upheaval caused by the war. Nine of the twenty-three prewar obkom first secretaries resumed their posts, and several of the remainder were transferred to new assignments in the Ukraine. In two oblasts the vacant first secretaryships were filled by the former chairmen of the executive committee, and in three others they were filled by former second secretaries. At least six of the chairmen of the oblast executive committees returned to their old posts, while the vacant chairmanships in a number of instances were filled by former vice-chairmen or departmental directors from the same oblasts. Much more fragmentary information on other obkom posts indicates that there was a considerable degree of continuity of personnel in these offices as well. There is a strong suggestion that the Soviet regime deliberately reinstalled these leading officials in their earlier positions, perhaps to heighten the impression of the restoration of normal control or perhaps because it was felt that, being familiar with their provinces, they were best able to cope with the enormous tasks of economic reconstruction and of restoration of loyalty to the system. In several cases, official biographical statements concerning these men indicate that they held posts in the Red Army or in other territorial organizations until the "liberation" of the Ukrainian oblasts where they had been stationed before the war. They were then released from these duties to return to their former posts even though the war was still going on.[42]

In the lower levels of the apparatus, however, continuity was not so great. In Stalino oblast, 906 of the 1,073 secretaries of primary Party organizations were persons new to directing work—for the most part young Party members who had first received responsible Party assignments during the war.[43] Some of the new officials were given jobs in posts similar to those they had held in the military service. For example, the secretary of the Party unit of a tank battalion became director of political affairs for an MTS.[44] A number of the new officials of the apparatus appear to have sought assignment to areas in the Ukraine on the basis of personal contacts formed in the military service. For example, Boris Galin, in *Donbas Sketches*, relates how a propagandist, whose whole career had been in Komsomol and Party work, was, when demobilized, invited by his former regimental commander to go to the Donbas. The latter, by then a raikom first secretary, secured his friend's appointment as staff propagandist of the raikom.[45] That there should have been a considerable turnover in the lower ranks was to be expected, since the total number of Party members and candidates had considerably increased during the war. In 1949 Khrushchev stated that 460,835 Communists (over two-thirds of the total) had entered the Ukrainian organization on demobilization from the Red Army.[46] Since it had been stated during the war that an "absolute majority" of the members and candidates (numbering 521,078 in 1940) were fighting at the front, it is probable that the large figure cited by Khrushchev included a considerable number of persons enrolled before the war. Moreover, a considerable number of the "war" Communists proved to be too unfamiliar with Party requirements, or too uninterested, to be retained; by 1949 the total of members and candidates was only 163,000 greater than in 1940. Nevertheless, the immediate postwar influx of new and relatively poorly indoctrinated members imposed a severe additional strain on the apparatus.

According to Khrushchev, Stalin was so embittered by Ukrainian behavior during the war that he would have dissolved the Republic and exiled its population if there had been any place to send the forty millions.[47] As far as the reaction of the general population was concerned, Stalin may have had some grounds for his anger. Embittered by the years of totalitarian oppression and by its accompanying starvation of the masses and degradation of the individual, a large portion of the Ukrainians welcomed the Germans until their equally vicious behavior became apparent. Even after that, many, while openly or covertly resisting the Germans, endeavored to use the war situation to prevent the return of the Soviet regime.

Most available evidence indicates that, from the standpoint of the regime, the Party and state apparatus in the Ukraine, in contrast to the general population, responded well to the test of war. Few, if any, middle-level members defected to the enemy or even engaged in collaborationist activities after capture.[48] While this "loyalty" was due in considerable measure to the Nazi policy of killing all Communist officials, it is nevertheless true that large numbers of officials strove in the face of great difficulties to organize resistance or to evacuate essential industry. While a state of panic seems to have prevailed during the first weeks, the later stages of the war found many officials—especially of the Party and the NKVD—sticking to their assigned posts until the last moment and returning behind the lines for extremely dangerous assignments. It should be noted, however, that the regime appears to have reserved the most desperate assignments, including the organization of underground forces, for less important members of the apparatus. The single exception to this rule, A. F. Fedorov, claims to have pleaded for the assignment.[49] Later, when such Party leaders as Korotchenko were dispatched behind the enemy lines, special measures were taken to ensure their safety, and their evacuation by air was provided after a short time. The regime was willing to risk its middle-level officials, but not to sacrifice them needlessly.

The general satisfaction of the regime with the reaction of the Ukrainian apparatus to the trial of war is indicated by the relatively high degree of continuity in leading posts, especially at the obkom level. In spite of the complete physical disruption of the apparatus caused by the occupation and in spite of the losses among personnel due to the war, the rate of turnover in major posts does not appear to have been significantly greater for the 1941-1944 period than in other periods of the same length since 1938, and the rate is far lower than the wholesale replacement incident to the Purge of 1937-1938. Undoubtedly the regime felt that restoration of stable control could be better achieved by avoiding a new disruption of the ruling apparatus; at the same time there can be little doubt that Stalin and his henchmen felt that this apparatus had served their purposes adequately during the war.

Footnotes to Chapter 9

[1.] Aleksei Fedorov, *The Underground Committee Carries On* (Moscow: Foreign Languages Publishing House), pp. 46 ff.; Aleksandr Nikolaevich Saburov, *Za linieiu frontu* [Behind the Front Line] (L'vov: Knyzhkovo-zhurnal'ne Vydavnytstvo, 1953), p. 12.

[2.] *PU*, February 5, 1949.

[3.] *PU*, October 17, 1951. While a number of high officials from the Ukraine served at fronts operating in or near Ukrainian territory, the overall national composition of these military commands does not appear to have differed significantly from that of the Red Army as a whole. According to *Bolshevik*, No. 6, 1944, 146 Ukrainians (about eighteen per cent of the total, compared to seventy-two per cent of Russians) had received awards of "Hero of the Soviet Union" on the First Ukrainian Front. The percentage of Ukrainians receiving the award in the entire Army up to October, 1944, was about sixteen, as compared to sixty-four per cent Russians. Cf. Julian Towster, *Political Power in the U.S.S.R., 1917-1947* (New York: Oxford University Press, 1948), p. 357.

[4.] *RU*, December 13, 1954; *PU*, October 3, 1944.

[5.] Natan Rybak, *Oruzhie s nami* [Arms with Us] (Moscow: Izdatel'stvo TsK VKSM "Molodaia Gvardiia, " 1944), p. 10, has Khrushchev himself tell one of Rybak's characters, a factory director, that his place is with his factory, which was to be evacuated, rather than in the army; Boris Galin in *Donbas Sketches* (Moscow: Foreign Languages Publishing House, 1948), cites many cases of important industrial officials who went east with their enterprises.

[6.] It is possibly significant that the Kemerovo assignment was not Zadionchenko's first major post in the R.S.F.S.R., for he had earlier been deputy chairman of its Council of People's Commissars.

[7.] *PU*, February 20, 1953.

[8.] See Chapter 7.

[9.] This section does not attempt to give a systematic account of the Red partisan movement in the Ukraine, or even a complete analysis of its relation to the Party and state apparatus. This problem—in the context of the entire Soviet partisan movement in World War II—has been the subject of an exhaustive series of accounts prepared by the War Documentation Project (a project administered by the Bureau of Applied Social Research, Columbia University, for the Department of the Air Force) and based in large part on captured German sources. The present writer is the author or co-author of a number of the sections of this series, which is classified as confidential; the titles may be found, however, in U. S. Department of State, Bureau of External Research, External Research Paper No. 122, "The German Occupation of the U.S.S.R. in World War II: A Bibliography," compiled by Alexander Dallin with the assistance of Conrad F. Latour, April 15, 1955 (mimeographed), p. 76. I have discussed a number of the military and political aspects of the partisans in the Ukraine in *Ukrainian Nationalism, 1939-1945* (New York: Columbia University Press, 1955).

[10.] Fedorov, p. 16.

[11.] Medvedev, p. 220.

[12.] NOKW 1519, a captured German document used in the trials of German war criminals by the U.S. Military Tribunal, Nuremberg.

[13] See "Eto bylo v Odesse" [It Was in Odessa], *Bol'shevistkoe Znamia,* February 2 and February 7, 1945.

[14] N. F. Kuz'min, *Kommunisticheskaia partiia—vdokhnovitel' i organizator bor'by ukrainskogo naroda za sozdanie i ukreplenie ukrainskogo sovetskogo gosudarstva* [The Communist Party—The Inspirer and Organizer of the Struggle of the Ukrainian People for the Creation and Strengthening of the Ukrainian Soviet State] (Moscow: Izdatel'stvo "Znanie," 1954), p. 34.

[15] *Ibid.*; Reports No. 6 and No. 7, "Einsatzgruppen der SP und des SD in der U.D.S.S.R." (No. 2658, U. S. Military Tribunal, Nuremberg).

[16] Kuz'min, p. 34; Mordukh Beniaminovich Pogrebinskii, "Trudiashchiesia Kieva i kievskoi oblasti v oborone stolitsy Ukrainskoi S.S.R." [The Toilers of Kiev and Kiev Oblast in the Defense of the Capital of the Ukrainian S.S.R.], an unpublished dissertation for obtaining the academic degree of candidate of historical sciences in the Academy of Sciences of the Ukrainian S.S.R., Kiev, 1953, p. 140.

[17] A. D. Kholodenin, "Kommunisticheskaia Partiia—vdokhovitel' i organizator borby trudiashchikhsia stalinskoi oblasti protiv nemetsko-fashistskikh zakhvatchikov (oktiabr' 1941-sentiabr' 1943 g.) [The Communist Party—the Inspirer and Organizer of the Struggle of the Toilers of Stalino Oblast Against the German-Fascist Aggressors (October 1941-September 1943)], an unpublished dissertation for obtaining the academic degree of candidate of historical sciences in the Kiev State University, 1956, p. 41.

[18] NOKW 1519.

[19] Fedorov, pp. 18-23.

[20] Kholodenin, p. 42.

[21] Cf. *Ibid.*, p. 43, for a Soviet admission of this circumstance.

[22] *Ibid.*, p. 52. This arrangement seems to have paralleled that of the Soviet partisan movement as a whole, where the Party official, P. K. Ponomarenko, was chief of the Central Staff of the Partisan Movement (formed on May 30, 1942), with K. Voroshilov as commander.

[23] Aleksandr Ruzanov in *Krakivs'ki Visti,* October 23, 1943, p. 3; Fedorov, p. 510.

[24] Marko Danilovich Lizogub, "Stanislavschchyna v period velikoï vitchysnianoï viiny (1941-1945 rr.)" [The Stanislav Area in the Period of the Great Fatherland War (1941-1945)], an unpublished dissertation for the academic degree of candidate of historical sciences, Stanislav, State Pedagogical Institute, 1951.

[25] P. Vershigora, *Liudi s chistoi sovest'iu* [People with Clean Consciences] (Moscow: Sovetskii Pisatel', 1951, rev. ed.), p. 203.

[26] Kholodenin, pp. 44-48.

[27] In May, 1940, there were 521,078 Party members and candidates—about 1.3 per cent of the population. If children and women (of whom only a small proportion were Communists) are excluded, one may estimate the Communist proportion of adult males as about 4 per cent. In the age group 17-40, from which most partisans apparently came, the proportion was undoubtedly much higher. The 1,721,000 Komsomols (in May, 1940) comprised 4.3 per cent of the total population, and probably over one-eighth of the males in the age group just referred to. Communists continued to predominate among underground agents, however; the Voroshilovgrad obkom dispatched 780 Communists and 360

140   *The Soviet Bureaucratic Elite*

Komsomols to the underground organization formed when its oblast was evacuated in the summer of 1942. Significantly, the same source states that the obkom sent 661 "persons" to partisan detachments at that time. See R. I. Novoplianskaia, "Bor'ba trudiashchikhsia voroshilovgradskoi oblasti protiv nemetskofashistskikh okkupantov (iiul' 1932-1943 g.)" [The Struggle of the Toilers of Voroshilovgrad Oblast Against the German-Fascist Occupiers (July, 1942-1943)], an unpublished dissertation for the academic degree of candidate of historical sciences in the Academy of Sciences of the Ukrainian S.S.R., Kiev, 1954, p. 36.

28. There have been persistent rumors in émigré circles that a large number of partisans—rank-and-file and lower officers—who did not adjust easily to the resumption of strict military or Party discipline after the relatively irregular life of the partisans during the early part of their activity were liquidated. Certain episodes in the Soviet partisan memoirs (see, for example, Fedorov, pp. 247, 261) suggest that this may indeed have been the case in many instances.

29. "25 let 'Radians' koï Ukraïny' " [Twenty-five Years of *Radians'ka Ukraïna*], *Bol'shevistskoe Znamia*, July 15, 1945; *Pravda*, November 8, 1941.

30. Fedorov, pp. 510-511 (referring to the autumn of 1942).

31. N. A. Savchuk, Rector of the University of Odessa. "Slava tebe velikii ruskii narod!" [Hail to Thee, Great Russian People!], *Bol'shevistskoe Znamia*, December 5, 1946.

32. Review by L. Pervomaiskii of "Partizany v stepakh Ukrainy" [Partisans in the Steppes of the Ukraine], a new film, in *Pravda*, March 6, 1943.

33. *Krasnaia Bashkiriia*, June 8 and 29, 1943.

34. Institute of Economics of the Academy of Sciences of the Ukrainian S.S.R., *Ocherki razvitiia narodnogo khoziaistva Ukrainskoi S.S.R.* [Essays on the Development of the National Economy of the Ukrainian S.S.R.] (Moscow: Izdatel'stvo Akademii Nauk S.S.S.R., 1954), pp. 453-455.

35. According to the announcement of Korniiets at the celebration in Moscow of the twenty-fifth anniversary of the formation of the Ukrainian S.S.R., *Pravda*, December 26, 1942.

36. Anatolii Shyian, *Partyzans'kyi Krai* [Partisan Territory] (Kiev: Ukraïns'ke Derzhavne Vydavnytsvo, 1946), pp. 3-4.

37. Ia. Tsvetov, "Khar'kov v eti dni" [Kharkov These Days], *Pravda*, February 28, 1943.

38. *Pravda*, August 31, 1943.

39. *Pravda*, September 9, 1943.

40. *Pravda*, September 18, 1943.

41. See, for example, *PU*, December 1, 1944, on the resumption of work of the Party cabinet in Zhitomir; and *Pravda*, December 3, 1943, concerning a meeting presided over by Serdiuk, the Kiev obkom first secretary, shortly after the reconquest. Khrushchev, as a member of the Military Council of the First Ukrainian Front, is said to have entered Kiev as soon as the Red Army did; he was quickly followed by the city, Party, and state officials. See V. A. Stepanov and M. I. Golyshev, *V boiakh za Dnepr* [In Battles for the Dnieper] (Moscow: Voennoe Izdatel'stvo Ministerstva Oborony Soiuza S.S.R., 1954), p. 78.

42. See, for example, the obituary of Filipp Timofeivich Sobko in *PU*, October 3, 1944; and of Kirill Leont'evich Bilyi, *PU*, August 22, 1951.

43. *PU*, August 8, 1944.

44. Mikhail Khomenko, "Zastupnyi direktor MTS" [The Deputy Director of the MTS], *RU*, April 20, 1947.

45. Galin, pp. 124-138.

46. Speech to Sixteenth Congress, *PU*, January 27, 1949. This may be compared to the proportion of sixty-two per cent of the Nikopol' city Party members who had entered during the war; see *PU*, November 26, 1946.

47. Khrushchev's secret speech to the Twentieth Party Congress (U. S. Department of State version, *The New York Times*, June 5, 1956).

48. See Armstrong, p. 243.

49. Fedorov, p. 16.

10

A New Oligarchy?

PERHAPS the most striking impression which emerges from a close examination of the Ukrainian apparatus is the diversity within this outwardly monolithic structure. No doubt the dissection of any organization produces something of this effect; but it does seem clear that all the efforts of totalitarianism have not succeeded in producing uniformity even within the ruling nucleus of the regime.

Diversity does not necessarily mean weakness. In some circumstances, indeed, it may be a sign of dynamism rather than decay. The elaborate mechanism for training the bureaucratic elite would certainly appear to be an element of strength. The constantly rising level of the officials' general education makes for efficient performance in an increasingly complex technological society. The rising proportion of high officials with advanced technical training contributes still more directly to this end. At the same time, the care of the Party to provide renewed ideological indoctrination at each stage of Party training acts as a powerful safeguard for continued loyalty.

Even the rising educational level of the elite is not an unmixed advantage for the regime, however. Whether or not education— assuming a certain admixture of general, quasi-humanistic study— is in itself dangerous for a totalitarian regime remains an unsettled question, although numerous direct observers of Soviet conditions believe it is.

Aside from this general question, there is a special reason why the rising level of education among the elite may cause difficulties for the Soviet system. The dominant group at present is still composed of the "men of '38," the voluntary or involuntary beneficiaries of the Purge. In general, members of this group had little formal education in their youth. They are men who rose "from the ranks" through practical ability and political cunning. Though all have received training in the Party schools and some have attained a high level of technical education, the longer periods of study usually came after the elite members were already well established in official careers. Training was a supplementary qualification, rather than a prerequisite for bureaucratic success. Consequently, this group is less likely to have developed a spirit of superiority from passing through selective training schools than is the group which entered the apparatus after the war. While the Party still requires alternation of practical experience with training for leadership, the aspirant must now be considerably younger for admission to the select Party schools, and the general educational requirements are much higher. Consequently, opportunities for education at a fairly early age now appear to be a prerequisite for a successful apparatus career. It would not be surprising if the newer group of leaders felt superior in qualifications to those who still dominate the apparatus, while the older leaders may well resent the relatively smooth road to success which the new men have followed. In the years immediately ahead there appears to be a distinct possibility of tension, if not a real "conflict of generations."

The heightened level of education is closely related to the factor of mobility. Until recently the Soviet Party and state elite has undoubtedly been one of the most mobile political groups in modern history. The decreased access to official careers and the slower promotion within the apparatus, which might have been anticipated after the consolidation of the Revolution, were postponed by the Great Purge, which swept away the top and middle strata of the elite. Since 1938 there has been no comparable replacement of the elite. War losses at the middle level of the apparatus were not very great. Nevertheless, the practice of replacing officials after an average of less than three years' service in major posts has been continued. As long as this practice remains in effect, there will continue to be ample room for promotion. The post-Purge group is now reaching an age level at which, given the early mortality of Soviet officials, frequent deaths may be anticipated and many high posts will become open. In the short run, therefore, though a promising bureaucratic career must be launched at an earlier age, there is no evidence that the chances of promotion for the most successful will be greatly diminished.

The impact of the changing elite composition upon specific apparatus careers is complicated. There seems little doubt that the line officials—the first secretaries and executive committee chairmen—will continue to be the most powerful figures in the Ukrainian apparatus. There is no reason to expect a recurrence of the immediate prewar situation in which Burmistenko's influence gave a special position to the staff agencies. The staff officials will probably continue to be closely associated with the line officials in a subordinate, auxiliary capacity. The increasing education of the line officials probably tends to bring them into closer contact with the staff officials, who at one time had superior formal training. At the same time, of course, it reduces the advantage the staff officials may have had two decades ago.

The relation of both line and staff officials to the indoctrination arm is less easily predicted. No doubt one source of friction between these groups has been the tendency of the post-Purge line official, with little formal training, but much practical experience in "direct action" involving difficult economic tasks and dangerous political operations, to scorn the expert in words. Increased formal training of line officials may inculcate more sympathy for the indoctrination group. On the one hand, the new line official is most frequently an engineer or other economic specialist: this group is not noted for its sympathy for activities which deal primarily with words rather than things.

The observations up to this point apply to the state and Party apparatus, which has been the principal object of this study. It is clear that career divisions within both the state bureaucracy and the Party bureaucracy are much more significant than the division between these bureaucracies. In fact, there is such a high degree of interchange between the middle levels of the state and Party bureaucracies that it is impossible to look upon these organizations as separate elite segments. Moreover, the principal line officials of both state and Party are so closely associated by both training and career as to constitute a single body.

The Party-state grouping already appears to extend to some degree to the industrial manager group; the whole complex of Party, state, and management in the Donbas coal region, for example, seems to have formed a partially distinct unit before 1953. As the proportion of technically trained and experienced state and Party line officials increases, their tendency to combine with industrial management in a number of technocratic groups formed on regional or economic bases may well increase.[1] Up to now, however, the dominant group of Party leaders who rose to power in 1938 has strongly resisted such a tendency. Certainly the rallying of territorial Party officials behind Khrushchev in June, 1957, and the subsequent demotion of several of the most prominent officials of the industrial manager type, indicates that the present oligarchy is a long way from being a technocracy. As for Khrushchev himself, he took his stand on this matter long ago:

> The Party is responsible for everything. Whether it is Army work, Chekist work, economic work, Soviet work—all is subordinate to the Party leadership, and if anyone thinks otherwise, that means he is no Bolshevik.[2]

Primacy for the Party has not, however, meant that the older leaders have avoided cross-institutional groupings; but Party men like Khrushchev have insisted on their own dominance in such alignments. Such seems to have been the complexion of the association between segments of the Party-state apparatus and the MVD. Certainly the events surrounding Lavrenti Beria's bid for power and his downfall demonstrate that at least two divergent groups existed in the police bureaucracy, one of which was willing to subordinate itself to the Party group headed by Khrushchev. While personal antagonisms may have been the predominant element in causing this group to oppose Beria and his cohorts, differences in training and in career experience between the frontier guard group associated with T. A. Strokach and the secret police adherents of Beria's minion, P. I. Meshik, were probably important. The close association of MVD and Party secretaries in frontier oblasts—mostly "men of '38," like V. A. Begma—probably played a part in inducing the frontier police to side with the Party group dominated by Khrushchev's adherents.

Types of training, career lines, and association in common activities tend to form cross-institutional alignments which, as power groups, may often be more important than formal structural divisions. These alignments, as the speculation concerning the police officials suggests, center around personal affiliations. In a sense the Soviet system is a vast collection of personal followings, in which the success of middle-level officials depends on the patronage of dominant leaders. An enormous variety of factors affects the links between a secondary official and the figure who acts as his patron. Many of these, undoubtedly, are so accidental in origin and so individual in nature that it will never be possible to trace fully such factors for any considerable number of officials. The element which could be most frequently determined is association in earlier assignments. Such association usually arises in the course of training or in assignment to posts in related areas of the apparatus. As previously noted, these related areas are as likely to be segments of different bureaucracies as divisions of the same formal structure. In most cases, the individual associations are part of a pattern of alignment between career groups such as those described above. Such associations, which arise as part of a larger career pattern, appear to have a greater chance of continuing than have purely chance associations arising from isolated individual contacts.

A major difficulty in estimating the role of the personal groupings in the Soviet system arises from the fact that they, like the institutional structures, tend to form pyramids with apexes beyond the Ukraine. The apex of each pyramid has been a major leader such as Andrei Zhdanov, Lavrenti Beria, and Georgi Malenkov; the pattern of associations leading to this patron lies in large part outside the scope of this study. Consequently, great caution has been exercised in speculating on the relation of the detectable cross-institutional groupings to personal power groups.

Because of his long career at the head of the Ukrainian apparatus, the followers of Nikita Khrushchev form a much more clearly discernible group. To a very important degree this apparatus as a whole has formed the base of Khrushchev's rapidly increasing power. Within the apparatus, however, it is possible to detect differences among segments and among individuals in degree of adherence to Khrushchev. Some suggestions along this line have been made earlier, especially in regard to the police machine and the Donbas managers. Within the Party-state apparatus itself, it seems clear that Khrushchev's closest associates are those who rose to positions of major importance while he was first secretary in the Ukraine. This applies especially to those who attained important posts after the war. Since the time when Khrushchev became First Secretary of the CPSU in April, 1953, and especially since the resignation of Malenkov as Premier in January, 1955, an increasing number of officials who rose to importance in the Ukrainian apparatus under Khrushchev have been transferred to major posts in other parts of the Soviet Union. The most prominent (all elected candidates or full members of the Central Committee of the CPSU at the Twentieth Congress) are the following:

V. M. Churaev, director of the Party Organs Section of the newly-formed Bureau of the CPSU for the Russian Republic—a key post for controlling the vast apparatus of this Russian Republic, now for the first time being treated as a unit of Party organization. Churaev had been a major obkom secretary and later he was deputy director of the major staff agency in the Ukrainian Party.

A. I. Kirichenko, Secretary of the Central Committee of the CPSU.

L. R. Korniets, Minister of Grain Products of the U.S.S.R., formerly a major figure in the Ukrainian Council of Ministers.

R. A. Rudenko, Procurator of the U.S.S.R., formerly in the corresponding post in the Ukraine.

A. P. Rudakov, apparently in a major industrial direction post, formerly director of the Heavy Manufacturing Section of the Central Committee of the KPU.

A. A. Epishev, Ambassador to Rumania, formerly first secretary of Odessa obkom.

A. P. Kirilenko, first secretary of Sverdlovsk obkom, a major

Siberian industrial area, formerly first secretary of Dnepropetrovsk obkom.

M. M. Stakhurskii, first secretary of Kharbarovsk Krai (Far
East), formerly first secretary of Poltava obkom.

V. S. Markov, first secretary of Orel obkom (European R.S.F.S.R.),
formerly first secretary of several Ukrainian obkoms.

A number of Khrushchev's former associates in the Ukraine,
though transferred somewhat earlier, were elected to the Central
Committee of the CPSU for the first time in 1956:

V. P. Mzhavanadze, first secretary of the Georgian S.S.R.,
formerly a major Soviet Army political officer in Kiev.

V. V. Matskevich, Minister of Agriculture of the U.S.S.R.,
formerly in the corresponding Ukrainian post.

A. I. Struev, first secretary of Molotov obkom, a major Ural
industrial center, formerly first secretary of Stalino obkom.

V. E. Semichastnyi, Secretary of the Komsomol of the U.S.S.R.,
formerly in the corresponding post in the Ukraine.

G. V. Eniutin, first secretary of Kamensk obkom (European
R.S.F.S.R.), formerly first secretary of Zaporozh'e obkom.

Khrushchev's use of the Ukrainian apparatus as a basis for extend-
ing his domination over wider spheres of the Soviet bureaucracies
is clearly suggested by the highly unusual number of major transfers
since 1954. This development is implicitly recognized by a Soviet
analysis, which says that the KPU has become "one of the most
important sources for the movement of cadres into the reserve of the
Central Committee of the CPSU," citing as examples some of the
officials listed above.[3] Taken together with the fact that nine members and six candidates of the Central Committee of the CPSU
elected in 1956 were drawn from officials serving at the time in the
Ukraine (as compared to four and five respectively in 1952), the
rapid increase in importance of officials drawn from the Ukrainian
apparatus is apparent.[4]

It would be incorrect to assume that the significance of the increase of importance of the Ukrainian apparatus is limited to the
enhancement of Khrushchev's personal power, important as Ukrain-

ian officials doubtless were in Khrushchev's victory in 1957. As
was pointed out earlier in this study, during Stalin's lifetime the
Ukrainian apparatus, together with apparatuses in some other
Republics, was distinguished from the CPSU central organization
by the regularity of its operations. At times this regularity appeared
through direct stress on adherence to rules in the routine work of
the Party. More important was the regular convocation of Party
assemblies called for in the Party regulations but ignored in the
CPSU during most of Stalin's rule subsequent to the Great Purge.
Party Congresses were somewhat more frequent in the Ukraine.
Much more important was the comparative frequency of Ukrainian
Central Committee sessions. The Central Committee of the KPU
met about four times a year—approximately as often as required by
the Party rules. There was, of course, no dissent on policy matters,
but a large proportion of the membership was present and spoke on
the topics considered.

All of these features indicate that "collective leadership" had
some meaning in the Ukraine even before Stalin's death; the principle itself was occasionally emphasized. There is no reason to at-
tribute this circumstance to any anti-dictatorial tendencies of
Khrushchev and his successors as first secretaries, or even to the
assertive qualities of other important officials. Quite as likely Stalin
deliberately encouraged some measure of collective rule in the
Ukraine in order to prevent this extremely important region from
falling under the domination of a single proconsul, who might have
used it as the base for opposition to the director. The importance of
the Ukrainian obkom secretaries in comparison to the Republic
Party leadership also contributed to dissemination of power.

Whatever the reasons for the peculiarities of Ukrainian apparatus
operation before 1953 as compared to other segments of the Soviet
apparatus, they did tend toward the oligarchic, as contrasted to the
autocratic, system of rule. In the years since Stalin's death a similar
development has taken place in the U.S.S.R. as a whole, but for
quite different reasons. As early as September, 1954, an important
Party publica. n, apparently strongly under Khrushchev's influence, sharply criticized irregularity of Party meetings during the
war period.[5] At the Twentieth Congress, when Khrushchev had

become still more powerful, the failure to hold regular Party meetings formed a major theme in the denunciation of the "cult of
personality." The special interest of the territorial apparatus in
stressing this theme became obvious when the Party journal *Kommunist* pointed out that local Party organizations, unlike the central
agencies, had held regular meetings in which "collective leadership"
was exercised even under Stalin's dictatorship.[6] By emphasizing its
role as a refuge for Leninist purity in a period of general degeneration
of Party practice, the territorial apparatus was, in effect, asserting
its claim to be the guide in present Party operations.

The simultaneous stress on regularity of Party operations and the
rise in influence of officials who had made their careers in the Ukrainian apparatus does not appear to be entirely coincidental. Probably the most important reasons why the present oligarchy has
preferred Khrushchev as leader are his quality as a representative Party boss, his relatively advanced age (which may lessen his
desire for absolute authority), and, of course, his ability as a "politi-
cian" in the popular sense of the word. It is also conceivable that
the "collective leadership" is familiar with Khrushchev's record of
regular operation of the Ukrainian Party and is consequently re-
assured that he will not hinder the development of oligarchic forms
of rule.

It is more probable that the attitudes and experience of the
Ukrainian elite members, developed over a long period of years, enable them to fit more smoothly into the present oligarchic system
than can many prominent officials from other segments of the apparatus in the U.S.S.R. Officials with experience in the Ukraine
can also use it as a working model for operating as an oligarchy on
an all-Union scale. To the extent that these factors are present, the
increase in importance of the Ukrainian apparatus elite means a
strengthening of oligarchic control of the U.S.S.R.

Footnotes to Chapter 10

¹· Cf. Barrington Moore, Jr., *Terror and Progress, U.S.S.R.* (Cambridge, Mass.: Harvard University Press, 1954), pp. 223-225.

²· Speech to the Fifteenth Party Congress, *Kolhospnyk Ukraïny*, May 20, 1940.

³· I. T. Pinegin, "Rabota KP Ukrainy po osushchestvleniiu reshenii partii o podbore, rasstanovke i vospitanii rukovodiashchikh partiinykh i sovetskikh kadrov v poslevoennyi period (1946-1955 gg.)" [The Work of the Communist Party of the Ukraine in Carrying Out the Decisions of the Party Concerning the Selection, Assignment, and Training of Directing Party and Soviet Cadres in the Postwar Period (1946-1955)], an unpublished dissertation for obtaining the academic degree of candidate of historical sciences in the Academy of Social Sciences of the Central Committee of the CPSU, Moscow, 1955, p. 114. It is interesting to note that this dissertation was completed in an institute of the Central Committee of the CPSU, rather than in a Ukrainian school.

⁴· Other officials who rose to prominence in the Ukraine include I. A. Serov, head of the Soviet police; L. I. Brezhnev, now Secretary of the Central Committee of the CPSU, who had however attained a major All-Union position before Stalin's death; L. R. Mel'nikov, who has remained in a secondary post since his demotion in 1953; and the coal mining specialists, A. F. Zasiadko and A. N. Zademidko.

⁵· L. Slepov, *Mestnye partiinye organy: Lektsii prochitannye v Vyshei Partiinoi Shkole pri TsK KPSS, Kafedra Partiinogo Stroitel'stva* [Local Party Organs: Lectures delivered in the Higher Party School of the Central Committee of the CPSU, Department of Party Structure] (Moscow: Vyshaia Partiinaia Shkola pri TsK KPSS, 1954), p. 19.

⁶· "Za tvorcheskuiu razrabotku istorii KPSS" [For Creative Reworking of the History of the CPSU], *Komunist*, No. 10, July, 1956, p. 23.

Bibliography

T̲HE principal body of source material for this study consists of Soviet publications—newspapers, periodicals, books—and unpublished Soviet dissertations. In addition, a large number of non-Soviet works on the Soviet Union and of general works in history, political science, and sociology have been used. A small number of captured German documents collected for the trial of war criminals at Nuremberg have been utilized. Finally, discussions with émigrés from the Ukraine and with Soviet Ukrainians have been helpful in clarifying many points.

The Soviet written sources have provided direct information on a large majority of the topics treated. Usually, the source of such information is specifically cited in the chapter notes. In addition, these sources have been used to construct a biographical file of approximately 2,400 entries. This file has formed the basis for tracing the careers of most of the individual officials discussed in the text and has provided the basis for much of the statistical analysis of career patterns. While all Soviet sources have been utilized to construct the biographical file, the newspapers, because of their more frequent reference to individual officials, have been by far the most important sources. Needless to say, it has been impossible to note the large number of sources used to construct the career biographies of each official.

*Newspapers**

Bolshevistskoe Znamia [Bolshevik Banner], Odessa, August-February, 1945 (gaps); 1946 (scattered numbers).
Izvestia [News], Moscow, 1937-1944 (substantially complete).
Kolhospnyk Ukraïny [Collective Farm Worker of the Ukraine], Kiev, May, 1939-February, 1941 (substantially complete).
Kommunist [Communist], Kiev,** October, 1939-September, 1941 (minor gaps); 1942 (scattered numbers).

---

* All newspapers were examined in the Library of Congress or in the New York Public Library. Files in these libraries frequently duplicate each other.
** These papers were published in various locations after the evacuation of Kiev in September, 1941. (See Chapter 7).

Krasnaia Bashkiriia [Red Bashkiria], Ufa, June-December, 1943 (scattered numbers).

Krasnaia Zvezda [Red Star], Moscow, September-December, 1939; June-July, 1940 (substantially complete).

Osvita [Education], Kiev, June-August, 1940 (gaps).

Pravda [Truth], Moscow, 1937-1956 (substantially complete).

Pravda Ukrainy [Truth of the Ukraine], Kiev, August, 1944-December, 1956 (substantially complete). Referred to in chapter notes as *PU*.

Radians'ka Ukraïna [Soviet Ukraine], Kiev, August, 1944-December, 1956 (substantially complete, except for 1951, fragmentary; and late March-early May, 1952, missing). Referred to in chapter notes as *RU*.

Sotsialisticheskii Donbass [Socialist Donbas], Stalino, February, 1940 (scattered numbers).

Sovetskaia Ukraina [Soviet Ukraine], Kiev,** 1941 (scattered numbers).

Stalinskoe Plemia [Stalinist Generation], Kiev, October, 1939-May, 1940; January-February, 1941 (gaps).

Tvarynnytstvo Ukraïny [Animal Husbandry of the Ukraine], Kiev, December, 1939-June, 1940 (gaps).

Vecherniaia Moskva [Evening Moscow], Moscow, July, 1936-December, 1937 (substantially complete).

Visti Rad Deputativ Trudiashchykhsia U.S.S.R. [News of the Soviet of Workers' Deputies of the Ukrainian S.S.R.], Kiev, January, 1937-April, 1941 (gaps). Referred to in footnotes as *Visti*.

Newspapers "spot-checked" only *

Komunist [Communist], Erivan, Armenian S.S.R.

Sovetskaia Belorussia [Soviet Belorussia], Minsk, Belorussian S.S.R.

Sovetskaia Kirgiziia [Soviet Kirgizia], Frunze, Kirgiz S.S.R.

Turkmenskaia Iskra [Turkmen Spark], Ashkhabad, Turkmen S.S.R.

Periodicals **

Bil'shovyk Ukraïny [Bolshevik of the Ukraine], Kiev, 1938-April, 1941 (some numbers missing).

Bolshevik [Bolshevik], Moscow, 1938-1944 (substantially complete).

* See Chapter 1, n. 9.
** Examined in the Library of Congress, the New York Public Library, Columbia University Library, and the University of Chicago Library.

154 The Soviet Bureaucratic Elite

Kolhospnytsia Ukraïny [Woman Collective Farm Worker of the Ukraine], Kiev, 1938 (some numbers missing).

Partiinaia Zhizn' [Party Life], Moscow, 1947-1948 (some numbers missing).

Partiinoe Stroitel'stvo [Party Construction], Moscow, 1938-1943 (some numbers missing).

Partiino-Politicheskaia Rabota v RKKA [Party-Political Work in the Workers-Peasants Red Army], Moscow, September, 1939-1940 (some numbers missing).

Radians'ka Osvita [Soviet Education], Kiev, 1940 (scattered numbers).

Radians'ka Zhinka [Soviet Woman], Kiev, 1947 (scattered numbers).

Radians'kyi Kyïv [Soviet Kiev], Kiev, May, 1939-December, 1941 (some numbers missing).

Radians'kyi L'viv [Soviet L'vov], L'vov, November, 1945-June, 1947 [scattered numbers).

Unpublished Soviet Dissertations*

Boldyrev, Nikolai Alekeseevich. "Bor'ba kommunisticheskoi partii za marksistsko-leninskoe vospitanie kadrov v gody tret'ei piatiletki (1938-1941 gg.). Na materialiakh Ukrainy." [The Struggle of the Communist Party for the Marxist-Leninist Training of Cadres in the Years of the Third Five-Year Plan (1938-1941). From Materials of the Ukraine]. Unpublished dissertation for obtaining the degree of candidate of historical sciences in the Department of Marxism-Leninism, Kiev State University, 1955.

Dem'ianchuk, Ivan Luk'ianovich. "Presa pidpil'nykh partiinykh orhanizatssi i partyzans'kykh zahoniv Ukraïny v borot'bi proty fashysts'kykh zaharbnykiv (1941-1944 rr.)" [The Press of the Underground Party Organizations and the Partisan Detachments of the Ukraine in the Struggle Against the Fascist Invaders (1941-1944)]. Unpublished dissertation for obtaining the academic degree of candidate of historical sciences in the Academy of Sciences of the Ukrainian S.S.R., Institute of History, Kiev, 1953.

Faians, Nataliia Isaakovna. "Sovetskaia gosudarstvennia sluzhba na sovremennom etape." [The Soviet State Service at the Present Stage]. Unpublished dissertation for obtaining the academic degree of candidate of juridical sciences in the All-Union Institute of Juridical Sciences, Moscow, 1955.

* Examined in the Lenin State Library, Moscow.

Fateev, Ivan Andreevich. "Bor'ba Kommunisticheskoi Partii, Sovetskogo Soiuza za povyshenie bditel'nosti sovetskogo naroda v poslevoennyi period (1945-1953 gg.)" [The Struggle of the Communist Party of the Soviet Union for Heightening the Vigilance of the Soviet People during the Postwar Period (1945-1953)]. Unpublished dissertation for obtaining the academic degree of candidate of historical sciences in the Department of History of the CPSU, Kiev State University, 1954 (revised 1956).

Fomin, I. A. "Podbor, rasstanovka i vospitanie rukovodiashchikh kadrov partiinogo i sovetskogo apparata v period mezhdu XIX i XX s"ezdami KPSS." [The Selection, Assignment, and Training of Directing Cadres of the Party and Soviet Apparatus in the Period Between the Nineteenth and the Twentieth Congresses of the CPSU]. Unpublished dissertation for obtaining the academic degree of candidate of historical sciences in the Department of History of the CPSU, Academy of Social Sciences of the Central Committee of the CPSU, Moscow, 1956.

Kholodenin, A. D. "Kommunisticheskaia Partiia—vdokhnovitel' i organizator borby trudiashchikhsia stalinskoi oblasti protiv nemetsko-fashistskikh zakhvatchikov (oktiabr' 1941-sentiabr' 1943 g.)" [The Communist Party—the Inspirer and Organizer of the Struggle of the Toilers of Stalino Oblast Against the German-Fascist Aggressors (October 1941-September 1943)]. Unpublished dissertation for obtaining the academic degree of candidate of historical sciences in the Kiev State University, 1956.

Kozik, Pavel Zotovich. "Vidbudova ta rozvytok hospodarstva i kul'turnoho zhyttia drohobyts'koi oblasti pislia vyhanannia nimets'ko-fashysts'kykh zaharbnykiv (6.VIII.1944-1.I.1947)" [Restoration and Development of Economic and Cultural Life in Drogobych Oblast After the Driving Out of the German-Fascist Invaders (6 August 1944-1 January 1947)]. Unpublished dissertation for obtaining the academic degree of candidate of historical sciences in the Kiev State University (?), 1947 (?).

Kulik, Grigorii Ivanovich."Ukraïns'ki burzhuazni natsionalisty—liuti vorohy trudiashchykh" [The Ukrainian Bourgeois Nationalists—Fierce Enemies of the Toilers]. Unpublished dissertation for obtaining the academic degree of candidate of historical sciences in the Kiev State University, 1947.

Likhenko, M. D. "Bor'ba kommunisticheskoi partii Sovetskogo

Soiuza za ideino-politicheskoe vospitanie rukovodiashchikh partiinykh i sovetskikh kadrov (1946-1950 gg.). Na materialiakh Ukrainy." [The Struggle of the Communist Party of the Soviet Union for Idea-Political Education of Directing Party and Soviet Cadres (1946-1950). From Materials of the Ukraine]. Unpublished dissertation for obtaining the academic degree of candidate of historical sciences in the Institute for Improving the Qualifications of Teachers of Marxism-Leninism, Kiev State University, 1955.

Lizogub, Marko Danilovich. "Stanislavashchyna v period velikoï vitchysnianoï viiny (1941-1945 rr.)" [The Stanislav Area in the Period of the Great Fatherland War (1941-1945)]. Unpublished dissertation for the academic degree of candidate of historical sciences. Stanislav, State Pedagogical Institute, 1951.

Lomov, Grigorii Ivanovich. "Ustanovlenie i ukreplenie sovetskoi vlasti v zapadnoi Ukraine (1939-1941 gg.)" [Establishment and Strengthening of Soviet Power in the West Ukraine (1939-1941)]. Unpublished dissertation for obtaining the academic degree of candidate of historical sciences in the Institute of History of the Ukraine, Academy of Sciences of the Ukrainian S.S.R., L'vov, 1953.

Men'shov, M. D. "Bor'ba kommunisticheskoi partii za sozdanie i vospitanie partiinykh i sovetskikh kadrov v zapadnykh oblastiakh Ukrainskoi S.S.R. v chetvertoi piatiletke (1946-1950 gg.)" [The Struggle of the Communist Party for Creating and Training Party and Soviet Cadres in the Western Oblasts of the Ukrainian S.S.R. in the Fourth Five-Year Plan (1946-1950)]. Unpublished dissertation for obtaining the academic degree of candidate of historical sciences in the Institute for Improving the Qualifications of Teachers of Marxism-Leninism, Kiev State University, 1954.

Morgun, Grigorii Ivanovich. "Borot'ba trudiashchykh l'vivs'koï oblasti proty tymchasovoï nimets'koï okupatsiï." [The Struggle of the Toilers of L'vov Oblast Against the Temporary German Occupation]. Unpublished dissertation for the academic degree of candidate of historical sciences in the L'vov State University, 1948.

Nazarova, Liubov' Vasil'evna. "Bor'ba kommunisticheskoi partii za sozdanie i vospitanie kadrov sovetskoi intelligentsii v zapadnykh oblastiakh Ukrainy (1939-1950 gg.)" [The Struggle of the Communist Party for the Creation and Training of Cadres of

Soviet Intelligentsia in the Western Oblasts of the Ukraine (1939-1950)]. Unpublished dissertation for obtaining the academic degree of candidate of historical sciences in the Institute for Improving the Qualifications of Teachers of Marxism-Leninism, Kiev State University, 1954.

Novoplianskaia, R. I. "Bor'ba trudiashchikhsia voroshilovgradskoi oblasti protiv nemetsko-fashistskikh okkupantov (iiul' 1942-1943 g.)" [The Struggle of the Toilers of Voroshilovgrad Oblast Against the German-Fascist Occupiers (July 1942-1943)]. Unpublished dissertation for the academic degree of candidate of historical sciences in the Academy of Sciences of the Ukrainian S.S.R., Kiev, 1954.

Pinegin, I. T. "Rabota KP Ukrainy po osushchestvleniiu reshenii partii o podbore, rasstanovke i vospitanii rukovodiashchikh partiinykh i sovetskikh kadrov v poslevoennyi period (1946-1955 gg.)" [The Work of the Communist Party of the Ukraine in Carrying Out the Decisions of the Party Concerning the Selection, Assignment, and Training of Directing Party and Soviet Cadres in the Postwar Period (1946-1955)]. Unpublished dissertation for obtaining the academic degree of candidate of historical sciences in the Academy of Social Sciences of the Central Committee of the CPSU, Moscow, 1955.

Pogrebinskii, Mordukh Beniaminovich. "Trudiashchiesia Kieva i kievskoi oblasti v oborone stolitsy Ukrainskoi S.S.R." [The Toilers of Kiev and Kiev Oblast in the Defense of the Capital of the Ukrainian S.S.R.] Unpublished dissertation for obtaining the academic degree of candidate of historical sciences in the Academy of Sciences of the Ukrainian S.S.R., Kiev, 1953.

Tsarev, N. I. "Bor'ba kommunisticheskoi partii Ukrainy za vypolnenie reshenii TsK KPSS po ideologicheskim voprosam v 1946-1952 gg. (na materialiakh zap. oblastei U.S.S.R.)" [The Struggle of the Communist Party of the Ukraine for Fulfillment of the Decisions of the Central Committee of the CPSU on Ideological Questions in 1946-1952 (from Materials of the Western Oblasts of the Ukrainian S.S.R.)]. Unpublished dissertation for obtaining the academic degree of candidate of historical sciences in the Institute for Improving the Qualifications of Teachers of Marxism-Leninism, Kiev State University, 1954.

Zhadovets, V. I. "Deiatel'nost' kommunisticheskoi partii v oblasti dal'neishego ukrepleniia sovetskogo gosudarstvennogo apparata v

158   *The Soviet Bureaucratic Elite*

gody chetvertoi piatiletki (na materialiakh Ukrainskoi S.S.R.)"
[The Activity of the Communist Party in the Area of Further
Strengthening the Soviet State Apparatus During the Years of
the Fourth Five-Year Plan (from materials of the Ukrainian
S.S.R.)]. Unpublished dissertation for obtaining the academic
degree of candidate of historical sciences in the Institute for Im-
proving the Qualifications of Teachers of Marxism-Leninism,
Kiev State University, 1956.

Books

Armstrong, John A. *Ukrainian Nationalism, 1939-1945.* New York:
Columbia University Press, 1955.
Baykov, Alexander. *The Development of the Soviet Economic System.*
New York: The Macmillan Co., 1947.
Bienstock, Gregory, Solomon M. Schwarz, and Aaron Yugow.
Management in Russian Industry and Agriculture. New York: Oxford
University Press, 1944.
Brzezinski, Zbigniew K. *The Permanent Purge.* Cambridge, Mass.:
Harvard University Press, 1956.
Chernovenko, S. *Ukraïna do zhovtnevoï revoliutsiï i v roky radians'koï
vlasty* [The Ukraine Before the October Revolution and in the
Years of Soviet Power]. Kiev: Derzhavne Vydavnytstvo Polity-
chnoï Literatury U.R.S.R., 1951.
Dosvid propahandysts'koï roboty v partorhanizatsiiakh Ukraïny [Experience
of Propaganda Work in the Party Organizations of the Ukraine].
Kiev: Derzhavne Vydavnytstvo Politychnoï Literatury U.R.S.R.,
1955.
Evseev, I. F. *Narodnye Komitety Zakarpatskoi Ukrainy: Organy gosu-
darstvennoi vlasti (1944-1945)* [The People's Committees of Trans-
carpathian Ukraine: Organs of the State Power (1944-1945)].
Moscow: Gosudarstvennoe Izdatel'stvo Iuridicheskoi Literatury,
1955.
Fainsod, Merle. *How Russia is Ruled.* Cambridge, Mass.: Harvard
University Press, 1954.
Fedorov, Aleksei Fedorovich. *Podpol'nyi obkom deistvuet* [The Under-
ground Committee Carries On]. Moscow: Izdatel'stvo TsK
VLKSM "Molodaia Gvardiia," enlarged edition, 1954.
———. *The Underground Committee Carries on.* Moscow: Foreign
Languages Publishing House, 1952. (This is a translation of the
first part of Fedorov's memoirs, published in Russian in 1947.)

Galin, Boris. *Donbas Sketches.* Moscow: Foreign Languages Publishing House, 1948.

———. *Donbass vozrozhdaetsia* [The Donbas is Reborn]. Moscow: Izdatel'stvo VTsSPS Profizdat, 1947.

Granick, David. *Management of the Industrial Firm in the U.S.S.R.: A Study in Soviet Economic Planning.* New York: Columbia University Press, 1954.

Harcave, Sidney. *Structure and Functioning of the Lower Party Organizations in the Soviet Union.* Maxwell Air Force Base, Alabama: Human Resources Research Institute; Technical Research Report Number 23, January, 1954.

Harper, Samuel N. *Civic Training in Soviet Russia.* Chicago: University of Chicago Press, 1929.

Inkeles, Alex. *Public Opinion in Soviet Russia.* Cambridge, Mass.: Harvard University Press, 1950.

Institute of Economics of the Academy of Sciences of the Ukrainian S.S.R. *Ocherki razvitiia narodnogo khoziaistva Ukrainskoi S.S.R.* [Essays on the Development of the National Economy of the Ukrainian S.S.R.]. Moscow: Izdatel'stvo Akademii Nauk S.S.S.R., 1954.

Isaeva, K. *Tsvetushchaia Ukraina: ocherk o dokumental'nom fil'me* [The Flowering Ukraine: a Sketch of a Documentary Film]. Moscow: Goskinoizdat, 1952.

Kalnins, Bruno. *Der sowjetische Propagandastaat.* Stockholm: Tidens Förlag, 1956.

KPSU v resoliutsiiakh i resheniakh s"ezdov, konferentsii i plenumov TsK [The CPSU in Resolutions and Decisions of the Congresses, Conferences, and Plenums of the Central Committee], Vol. II. Moscow: Gosudarstvennoe Izdatel'stvo Politicheskoi Literatury, 1953.

Kuz'min, N. F. *Kommunisticheskaia partiia—vdokhnovitel' i organizator bor'by ukrainskogo naroda za sozdanie i ukreplenie ukrainskogo sovetskogo gosudarstva* [The Communist Party—the Inspirer and Organizer of the Struggle of the Ukrainian People for the Creation and Strengthening of the Ukrainian Soviet State]. Moscow: Izdatel'stvo "Znanie," 1954.

Lasswell, Harold D. *The Political Writings of Harold D. Lasswell.* Glencoe, Ill.: The Free Press, 1951.

Lasswell, Harold D., Daniel Lerner, and C. Easton Rothwell. *The Comparative Study of Elites.* Hoover Institute Studies, Series B: Elites, No. 1. Stanford: Stanford University Press, 1952.

Lialikov, N. I.   *Sovetskaia Ukraina: ocherk ekonomicheskoi geografii* [The Soviet Ukraine: A Sketch of Economic Geography]. Moscow: Gosudarstvennoe Izdatel'stvo Geograficheskoi Literatury, 1954.

Lisovin, A.   *Biblioteka gorkoma partii* [The Library of the Gorkom of the Party].   Moscow: Gospolitizdat, 1955.

Mannheim, Karl.   *Man and Society in an Age of Reconstruction.*   New York: Harcourt, Brace & Co., 1940.

Markus, Vasyl.   *L'Incorporation de l'Ukraine Subcarpathique à l'Ukraine Soviétique, 1944-1945.*   Louvain: Centre Ukrainien d'Etudes en Belgique, 1956.

Medvedev, Dmitrii.   *Sil'nye dukhom* [The Strong in Spirit].   Moscow: Voennoe Izdatel'stvo Voennogo Ministerstva Soiuza S.S.R., 1951.

Meissner, Boris.   *Russland in Umbruch.*   Frankfurt a/M: Verlag für Geschichte und Politik, 1951.

Min, D.   *Zapadnaia Ukraina* [The West Ukraine].   Moscow: Gosudarstvennoe Izdatel'stvo Politicheskoi Literatury, 1939.

Moore, Barrington, Jr.   *Soviet Politics: The Dilemma of Power.*   Cambridge, Mass.: Harvard University Press, 1950.

————.   *Terror and Progress, U.S.S.R.*   Cambridge, Mass.; Harvard University Press, 1954.

Nemec, Frantisek, and Vladimir Moudry.   *The Soviet Seizure of Subcarpathian Ruthenia.*   Toronto: William B. Anderson, 1955.

Ovechkin, Valentin.   *Z frontovym pryvitom: povist'* [Greetings from the Front: A Story].   Kiev: Vydavnytstvo "Radians'ka Ukraïna," 1946.

Pareto, Vilfredo.   *The Mind and Society.*   Edited by Arthur Livingston and translated by Arthur Livingston and Andrew Bonjorno. New York: Harcourt, Brace & Co., 1935.

Parsons, Talcott.   *The Social System.*   Glencoe, Illinois: The Free Press, 1951.

Partiinyi pratsivnyk—politychnyi kerivnyk [The Party Worker—A Political Leader].   Kharkov: Ukraïnske Derzhavne Vydavnytstvo, 1945.

Radians'ka Ukraïna ta A.M.S.R.R.: ekonomichno-adresovyi dovidnyk [The Soviet Ukraine and the Autonomous Moldavian Soviet Socialist Republic: An Economic-Address Directory].   Odessa: Vydannia Derzhnavnoho Vydavnytstva "Narodne Hospodarstvo ta Oblik," 1934.

Rybak, Natan. *Oruzhie s nami* [Arms With Us]. Moscow: Izdatel'-stvo TsK VLKSM "Molodaia Gvardiia," 1944.

Saburov, Aleksandr Nikolaevich. *Za liniieiu frontu* [Behind the Front Line]. L'vov: Knyzhkovo-Zhurnal'ne Vydavnytstvo, 1953.

Schwartz, Harry. *Russia's Soviet Economy.* New York: Prentice-Hall, 2nd ed., 1954.

Shyian, Anatolii. *Partyzans'kyi krai* [Partisan Territory]. Kiev: Ukraïns'ke Derzhavne Vydavnytsvo, 1946.

Slepov, L. *Mestnye partiinye organy: Lektsii prochitannye v Vyshei Partiinoi Shkole pri TsK KPSS, Kafedra Partiinogo Stroitel'stva* [Local Party Organs: Lectures Delivered in the Higher Party School of the Central Committee of the CPSU, Department of Party Structure]. Moscow: Vyshaia Partiinaia Shkola pri TsK KPSS, 1954.

Stepanov, V. A., and M. I. Golyshev. *V boiakh za Dnepr* [In Battles for the Dnieper]. Moscow: Voennoe Izdatel'stvo Ministerstva Oborony Soiuza S.S.R., 1954.

Towster, Julian. *Political Power in the U.S.S.R., 1917-1947.* New York: Oxford University Press, 1948.

Tsentralnoe Statisticheskoe Upravlenie pri Sovete Ministrov S.S.S.R. Narodnoe khoziastvo S.S.S.R.: statisticheskii sbornik [The National Economy of the U.S.S.R.: A Statistical Yearbook]. Moscow: Gosudarstvennoe Statisticheskoe Izdatel'stvo, 1956.

Ukraïns'ka R.S.R.: administratyvno-terytorialnyi podil na 1 veresnia 1946 roku [The Ukrainian S.S.R.: Administrative-Territorial Division on September 1, 1946]. Kiev: Ukraïns'ke Vydavnytstvo Politychnoï Literatury, 1947.

U. S. Department of State, Bureau of External Research, External Research Paper No. 122, *The German Occupation of the U.S.S.R. in World War II: A Bibliography.* Compiled by Alexander Dallin with the assistance of Conrad F. Latour, April 15, 1955 (mimeographed).

Vershigora, Peter. *Liudi s chistoi sovest'iu* [People With Clean Consciences]. First and Second Book. Moscow: Moskovskii Rabochii, 1946.

———. *Liudi s chistoi sovest'iu* [People With Clean Consciences]. Moscow: Sovetskii Pisatel', rev. ed., 1951.

Vsia Moskva: adresno-spravochnaia kniga, 1936 god. [All Moscow: An Address-Reference Book, 1936.] Moscow: Moskovskii Rabochii, '36.

Vucinich, Alexander. *Soviet Economic Institutions.* Stanford, California: Stanford University Press, 1952.

Weber, Max. *Grundriss der Sozialoekonomik.* 3rd ed. Tuebingen: J. C. B. Mohr, 1947.

Wolin, Simon and Slusser, Robert M., editors, *The Soviet Secret Police.* New York: Frederick A. Praeger, 1957.

Zapadnaia Belorussiia i zapadnaia Ukraina pod gnetom panskoi Pol'shi [West Belorussia and West Ukraine Under the Yoke of Aristocratic Poland].   Moscow: Gosudarstvennoe Voennoe Izdatel'stvo, v Voennogo Ministerstva Soiuza S.S.R., 1939.

Index

Academy of Sciences of the Ukrainian S.S.R., 35, 133
Administration for Verification of Party Organs, 85 *n. 7*
age:
    and conflict of generations, 143
    Communists of military age, 139 *n. 27*
    of "directing cadres," 22
    of elite, 26, 27
    of KPU Congress delegates, 21, 22
    of students in Party schools, 39, 40
    see also biographies of individual officials
Agitation and Propaganda Section of Komsomol Central Committee, 91, 95, 97
agricultural department, 62, 82
agricultural section, 62, 63
agriculture:
    collectivization of, 56, 61, 114-115
    line officials and, 49
    Party organization in, 61-64
    state bureaucracy and, 54
    Ukrainian Ministry of, 63, 64, 148
    U.S.S.R. Ministry of, 148
    weakness of, 61
Agriculture and Procurements: Ukrainian Ministry of, 63
agronomists, 64
Akkerman; *see* Belgorod-Dnestrovskii
Akkerman oblast; *see* Izmail
All-Union Ministries, 63, 64-66, 68-69
apparatus, 3-5
    defined, 3
Armenian Party Congresses, 29 *n. 9*
Army, 7, 127, 133, 134-135, 147
    and annexation of Polish areas, 106-109, 116, 117
    and demobilized Communists and officials, 135
    personnel in partisans, 129, 131
    political administration of, 73
    proportion of Ukrainians and Russians in, 138 *n. 3*

representation in KPU Central Committee, 15
subordination to Party, 145
training of officers, 44 *n. 24*
Ashkabad, 132
attrition; *see* turnover
Austria-Hungary, 109-120

Babiichuk, R. V., 101
Bairam Ali, 133
Bashkir A.S.S.R., 133
Begma, V. A., 117, 130, 145
Belgorod-Dnestrovskii, 124 *n. 27*
Belletristic and Art Affairs Section of KPU Central Committee, 92, 94, 97
Belogurov, N. K., 92, 94
Belorussian Party Congresses, 29 *n. 9*
Benes, Eduard, 108
Beria, Lavrenti, 121, 145, 146
Bessarabia, 106
Bogatyr', Z. A., 131
Bondar', I. I., 82
Borkaniuk, Aleksei, 124 *n. 22*
Brezhnev, L. I., 50-51, 151 *n. 4*
Briansk, 129
Bubnovskii, N. D., 70 *n. 10*
Bug River, 128
Bukovina, 106
Bureau:
    of CPSU for Russian Republic, 147
    of gorkom, 78, 79
    of obkom, 13, 14, 36, 62, 77
bureaucracy in Soviet Union:
    defined, 3, 9 *n. 7*
Burmistenko, M. A., 72-75, 84, 126, 129, 144
Butenko, G. P., 63, 71 *n. 11*

cabinet of gorkom, 79, 140 *n. 41*
cadres secretary, 74-78, 119, 130
    and MVD, 74
    in "family groups," 82
cadres section:
    and "family groups," 82
    and line officials, 78-79

Heavy Metallurgy:
  Ministry for, 68
Higher Party School of CPSU Central
  Committee, 34, 36, 38
  Correspondence Section of, 34
Higher Party School of KPU Central
  Committee:
  admission to, 37-39
  age of students, 39-40
  aims, 36-37
  curriculum, 35-37
  faculty, 35-37
  formation, 34, 37, 41, 121
  indoctrination officials and, 37
  information on, 43 *n. 12*
  officials enrolled in, 38
  size of student body, 37
  social origin of students, 40
  training of journalists, 92, 93
Hungary, 108-110, 124 *n. 22*

"ideological work"; *see* indoctrination
indoctrination:
  definition, 88
  in factories, 67
  in war, 127-128
  in West Ukraine, 107, 111
  of "war" Communists, 136
  oral, 90-91
  position of officials for, 96-101, 102,
    142, 144
  training of officials for, 37-40
"industrial branch" sections, 68, 75,
  80-81
industry, 64-69, 145
  in Dnepropetrovsk oblast, 50, 52
  in Kharkov oblast, 52
  in Siberia, 148
  in Stalino oblast, 51
  in Urals, 148
  in war, 127, 133, 136, 138 *n. 5*
  Moscow control of, 54
  obkom secretaries and, 49-50
  reorganization of control of, 68-69
inspectors of KPU Central Committee,
  74, 85 *n. 6*, 101
Institute for Improving the Qualifications of Teachers of Marxism-
  Leninism, Kiev University, 35

Institute of the Red Professors, 36
instructors, 33, 37, 79, 81
Internal Affairs:
  Ukrainian Ministry of; *see* MVD
Ivanichi, 118
Izmail, 49, 112, 113-114, 124 *n. 27*

Jews:
  and anti-Semitism, 18
  and Nazi extermination policy, 18
  as editors, 92
  in Kiev, 18
  in Party membership, 17-18
  in population of Ukraine, 17-18
  in West Ukraine, 105-106
  L. I. Troskunov as, 92
  Moisei S. Spivak as, 74, 85 *n. 4*
  Raisa Iu. Khomiakova as, 92
journalists, 40, 92-95, 103 *n. 11*, 103
  n. 13, 120
  see also editors

Kabychivka, 133
Kaganovich, Lazar M., 69
Kalashnikov, V. D., 63
Kalmyk, A.S.S.R., 73
Kamenets-Podolsk, 40
Kamensk, 148
Kazakh S.S.R., 51
Kemerovo, 127, 138 *n. 6*
Kharbarovsk, 148
Kharkov, 33, 40, 50, 52, 61, 75, 92-93,
  103 *n. 11*, 111, 129, 133, 134
Kharkov Communist Institute of
  Journalism, 92, 108
Kharkov Engineering-Construction
  Institute, 50
Kherson, 49, 58 *n. 5*
Khomiakova, Raisa Iu., 92
Khrushchev, Nikita S., 1, 2, 21, 30
  n. 19, 50, 54, 73, 100, 107, 135, 136,
  138 *n. 5*, 140 *n. 41*
  and "collective leadership," 148-150
  and economic control agencies, 69
  and indoctrination officials, 101
  and power struggle, 145-147
  and I. A. Serov, 55
  and staff agencies, 74-75
  as First Secretary of CPSU, 147, 150

and instructors, 80
and Party training, 38
and propaganda secretary, 89
coal section of, 51
"industrial branch" sections of, 68
in West Ukraine, 108, 109, 121
Party school of, 121
special section of, 98-99
underground, 49, 128-130
see also Bureau, cadres secretaries,
cadres section, organization-instruction section, Party organizations section, propaganda secretaries, propaganda section, second
secretaries, secretaries
oblast (province):
defined, 11
oblast executive committee, 62, 108,
109, 119, 120, 134
Ocheretianyi, V. T., 113
Odessa, 33, 51, 83, 97, 111, 114, 126,
127, 128, 147
Odessa University, 133
"Old Bolsheviks," 20
Oleinyk, Z. F., 127
oligarchy, 145, 149, 150
Olyka, 118
Orel, 129, 148
organization-instruction section, 72-
73, 75-76, 79
Organizational Bureau, 85 *n. 1*
organizer of the Central Committee;
see Central Committee of CPSU
Orgburo, 85 *n. 1*

Palamarchuk, L. F., 92
Panchishin, M. I., 119
Pareto, Vilfredo, 2
Partiins Zhittia, 90
partisans, 55-56, 74, 85 *n. 4*, 85 *n. 5*,
110, 117, 128-132, 138 *n. 9*, 139
n. 22, 139 *n. 27*, 140 *n. 28*
formation, 128
in L'vov area, 117
Party (Communist Party of the
Ukraine):
membership:
from Army, 135-136, 139 *n. 27*,
141 *n. 46*

in rural raions, 61
in underground and partisans,
128-129, 131
in West Ukraine, 115
see also Central Committee of KPU,
Congresses of KPU
Party College, 85 *n. 1*
Party Commission, 85 *n. 1*
Party organizations section:
and instructors, 80-81
formation, 75
in Party training, 79
Party Organs Section of Bureau of
CPSU for Russian Republic, 147
Party schools, 33, 34-35, 37, 39-40
Party, trade union, and Komsomol
organizations section; *see* Party organizations section
Party training:
age of admission to, 143
and propaganda sections, 94
effect on loyalty, 142
in gorkom cabinets, 79
in L'vov oblast school, 117
of cadres officials, 78
of journalists, 94-95, 103 *n. 11*
of staff officials, 144
relation to personal groupings, 146
Pavlograd, 39
peasantry; *see* kolkhoznike
Pelekhatyi, K. N., 120
People's Commissariat of Internal
Affairs (NKVD); *see* MVD
People's Committees, 108-109
Perets, 94
Perm; *see* Molotov oblast
personnel; *see* cadres, *nomenklatura*
officials
Petrushchak, I. D., 110
Pidtychenko, Mariia M., 28 *n. 2*, 41,
44 *n. 27*
biography of, 90
Pinchuk, G. P., 110
plant managers, 65, 66
see also managers
Platonov, M. A., 132
Podgornyi, N. V., 52
Poland, 116-117, 119-120, 126
see also West Ukraine